Holidays
For
KIDS

Holidays
For
KIDS

And Parents, Too!

Create Childhood Memories and Traditions
That Will Last a Lifetime

Charles Pascalar

Order this book online at www.trafford.com
or email orders@trafford.com

Most Trafford titles are also available at major online book retailers.

Printed in the United States of America.

ISBN: 978-1-4669-0546-7 (sc)
ISBN: 978-1-4669-0545-0 (hc)
ISBN: 978-1-4669-0547-4 (e)

Library of Congress Control Number: 2012904011

Trafford rev. 04/23/12

 www.trafford.com

North America & international
toll-free: 1 888 232 4444 (USA & Canada)
phone: 250 383 6864 ♦ fax: 812 355 4082

Over Fifty *Fun* Ideas

The *Most* Important Birthday
The Holiday They Will *Hate*
Awesome August Adventure Day
Opposite Day
One Day Fun Day
Popcorn Day
Presents Day
January Journey
May Day Play Day
September Search

Contents

Preface: Holidays for Kids

This book is about how to make your children's childhoods the best ever. All it really takes are two things: your love and your time. Your love will always be there, but because of myriad adult responsibilities, your time can slip away from you. This book offers ways to help you have *fun* with your kids, to enjoy your kids as they grow up, and to be a bigger part of their lives than ever before. It's also about teaching them and building their self-confidence so they can succeed as adults.

Parenting is a tremendous challenge; it's about starting with a baby who is 100 percent *dependent* on you and, over the subsequent eighteen years, making him or her 100 percent *independent* of you. There will be tension and trust, arguments and compromises, but these usually come in the teenage years. This book focuses on the childhood years (age twelve and under), when you are your child's whole world and you get to play the biggest role in his or her development.

My kids are just passing through their childhoods now. And, as I was writing this book, I asked them to remember the details I had forgotten of some of the holidays we celebrated. They could remember exactly what activities we did together and how we did them. Now, some of the specifics in this book were added because they just hit me while I was writing, and I wondered why I didn't think of them earlier.

Within each chapter, you will find that I created a theme that ties the activities into the holidays most people already celebrate in that particular season. By sticking to certain, definitive approaches and beliefs, these themes become ingrained in children's minds and must be followed each year. You can always change them for your own needs, but be prepared to explain why you are changing them. Kids remember everything.

A great many things we do as adults have origins in the teachings of our parents (whether we want to give them credit or not), and we often become our parents as we age. What better tradition to pass along to the next generation than a wonderful childhood filled with great times spent together? This book and the memories I created with my kids were a hit, and I hope they will be a hit for you too.

Please send me a note if you come up with new ideas that you enjoy or just to let me know how these ideas actually worked for you! Follow me on twitter @cpascalar.

January

Many of us start the new year a little numb after going through all the holiday hoopla. We might consider just letting the kids play with the toys they just got while the grown-ups rest a little bit, right?

Wrong!

January Journey

January 1

Let's start with a little fun with the leftover Christmas wrapping paper.

Whereas Christmas offered presents under the tree, visible to everyone and easily identified by name tags or color paper, this time the kids will go on a journey through the house, looking for their treasure.

After the excessiveness of Christmas, this will be low-key. It involves one present, wrapped and hidden, someplace in the house. This activity is really for kids who are a little older, as they have more patience than little ones do; and they are able to move around the house easily without direct supervision.

How do the kids know what to look for? Give them samples of the wrapping paper that you used to wrap their gifts, and those will serve as their clues. The present could be a book, a gift card (great for preteens), a doll, or whatever you like, but the fun should be in the search. Putting a wrapped book on a book shelf with only the spine showing is clever but, as I learned, too hard to find. The key is to hide it in an age-appropriate, moderately hard place to find. The younger the child, the easier it should be to find.

This simple game helps to teach perseverance and a timeless life lesson: when you try hard and don't give up, there is a reward at the end of the journey. And if you time it right, it will give you plenty of time to watch the football games on TV.

Start the Year with Lots of Good Luck!

Many believe that there are several foods that will bring good luck and improve the odds that the coming year will be great. According to epicurious.com, in an article entitled "Lucky Foods for the New Year," by Lauren Salkeld, "Traditions vary from culture to culture, but there are strikingly similar foods consumed for good luck in different pockets of the world—grapes, leafy greens, fish, pork, legumes, and cakes."

The similarity of many beliefs has to do with certain numbers. Eating twelve of something (one of each month) or 365 (one for each day) would be the way to ensure good luck for the entire year. My favorite is *cookies*!

Lauren Salkeid continues that "Around the world, cakes and other baked goods are commonly served from Christmas Eve to New Year's Day, with a special emphasis placed on round or ring-shaped goods. In certain cultures, it's customary to hide a special trinket or coin inside the cake—the recipient of the piece containing the item will be lucky in the new year. In Mexico, the *rosca de reyes* is a ring-shaped cake decorated with candied fruit and baked with one or more surprises inside. In Greece, a special round cake called *vasilopita* is baked with a coin hidden inside. At midnight, or after the New Year's Day meal, the cake is cut, with the first piece going to St. Basil, and the rest being distributed to guests in order of age. Sweden and Norway have similar rituals in which they hide a whole almond in rice pudding—whoever gets the nut is guaranteed great fortune in the new year."

My variation of the above was the eating of twelve cookies. Since many of my traditions involved foods, and more importantly, *my* favorite foods, I tried to weave them into my holidays so my wife would always be willing to buy these for me. My favorite cookies were Nilla wafers and Oreos. The eating of the cookies started out with the Nilla wafers, as they looked like gold coins to me, and it made sense to tie these into good fortunes. As time went on and double-stuffed Oreo cookies caught my taste buds, I switched to those because, since there were three layers to each cookie, it made sense we would get three times the good luck if we ate those!

The rest of this section discusses some cool customs from around the world from the previously referenced article that are far healthier than cookies. I was not above trying to convince my kids that twelve corn kernels, twelve green beans, and twelve pieces of meat were also part of the tradition, but the cookies stuck! Of course, they routinely point out to me that cookies are for good luck, and so we need to really stockpile them in the pantry to make extra sure we get our share of good fortune.

Grapes

"New Year's Eve revelers in Spain consume twelve grapes at midnight—one grape for each stroke of the clock."

Leafy Greens

"Cooked greens, including cabbage, collards, kale, and chard, are consumed at New Year's celebrations in different countries for a simple reason—their green leaves look like folded money and are considered to be symbolic of economic fortune."

Legumes

"Legumes including beans, peas, and lentils are also symbolic of money. Because they are small and round, they are said to resemble coins which swell when cooked; so they are eaten with financial rewards in mind. In the southern United States, it's traditional to eat black-eyed peas, or cowpeas, and there are even those who believe in eating one pea for every day of the New Year. This all traces back to the legend that, during the Civil War, the town of Vicksburg, Mississippi, ran out of food while under attack. The residents fortunately discovered black-eyed peas, and the legume was thereafter considered lucky."

Pork

"The custom of eating pork on New Year's is based on the idea that pigs symbolize progress. The animal pushes forward, rooting itself in the ground before moving."

Fish

"Fish is a very logical choice for the New Year's table." According to Mark Kurlansky, author of *Cod: A Biography of the Fish that Changed the World*, "cod has been a popular feast food since the Middle Ages.

He compares it to turkey on Thanksgiving. The reason? Long before refrigeration and modern transportation, cod could be preserved and transported, allowing it to reach the Mediterranean and even as far as North Africa and the Caribbean. Herring, another frequently preserved fish, is consumed at midnight in Poland and Germany—Germans also enjoy carp and have been known to place a few fish scales in their wallets for good luck. The Swedish New Year feast is usually a smorgasbord with a variety of fish dishes such as seafood salad. In Japan, herring roe is consumed for fertility, shrimp for long life, and dried sardines for a good harvest (sardines were once used to fertilize rice fields)."

And there were some foods to *avoid* so you wouldn't encourage bad luck for the new year. "Lobster, for instance, is a bad idea because they move backward and could therefore lead to setbacks. Chicken is also discouraged because the bird scratches backward, which could cause regret or dwelling on the past. Another theory warns against eating any winged fowl because good luck could fly away."

Resolutions

One of the most popular things to do for New Year's is something I gave up years ago. I confess that I really didn't want to lose weight, exercise, or eat better. Considering that I was eating twelve cookies for good luck, it goes without saying that starting a resolution at the same time was a bit of a problem. I did encourage my kids to make resolutions and try and work on something they should be better at, like homework, or being nicer to each other, or even helping Mom with some chores, but lack of willpower evidently runs in our family. Truthfully, after many years of failing to see my resolutions through, I started looking at things in a whole new way. So, like most of us, upon suffering agony after working out early in the new year and then giving up, I decided my resolutions were going to be things I *wanted* to do that year—read a particular book, learn to play the piano, take a vacation someplace special, write a book (Guess what my resolution was this year?), try all the top ten restaurants listed in my city's local magazine, paint a picture, or come up with a new holiday for my kids to enjoy.

Just think about what you've always wanted to do and make that *your* resolution. If your family does well with traditional resolutions, then stay the course and enjoy how well adjusted you are and be proud of your ability and perseverance.

Dreamer Day

The third Monday in January is a holiday recognizing the importance of Dr. Martin Luther King Jr. His efforts sparked a turning point in history and are still considered to be a triumph in the pursuit of civil rights. When I was in the seventh grade, I was one of two children who delivered a short speech on Dr. King, over the loudspeaker from the principal's office at Brockport Middle School, identifying and acknowledging his accomplishments. I remember how proud I felt when the principal congratulated me on being one of the two selected, and afterward I felt a little closer to Dr. King and this cause.

Dreamer Day is, of course, based on Dr. King's famous speech, "I Have a Dream," which he delivered on August 28, 1963, in Washington, DC. And the pride I felt upon being recognized when I was in the seventh grade is the foundation for this holiday. Dreamer Day is a day to encourage your kids to write about their own hopes and dreams and to recognize them for what they feel and how they voice those feelings.

This is for almost any age group, but certainly for school-age children. You might ask a few simple questions, if they need help getting started, such as:

> What is the perfect world?
> What makes you happiest?
> What is the best way to help other people?
> What do you dream about?
> What do you want to be when you grow up?
> Who would be the perfect person to marry?
> What would you name your children?

You can add to the list yourself, and then be prepared for a whole range of things to be thrown back at you. The point, though, is that this is your child's idea of what he or she thinks is interesting. Don't be alarmed if your child writes about eating donuts every day, having his or her bed made automatically, staying up late, or having Grandma live with you.

The subject of this project will change every year, and you will have the history of your children's thoughts, dreams, and ideas.

So, once your kids have written everything they want to say, it's important to take time to recognize their work. This is all about making a celebration of their accomplishments. Make sure they sign it!

Take them to the local store and have them choose frames for their works. Frame their pieces and put them in a place of prominence—not the refrigerator—such as a wall or countertop. It should be someplace they do not have to share, and it should be where the piece can remain until the following year. This helps them to know that their work is appreciated and that their ideas are acknowledged. The importance of what they think and believe helps set the stage for self-confidence! Each year, remove the previous document and replace it with the new one. But do keep the old one(s), and give them all back to your child when appropriate. You will see how this fits in with special birthdays later in the book.

As your children get older, and you want to show them the true spirit of Dr. King's words, you can volunteer to help the community. Reading his actual speech, and understanding it, can help your children develop a true appreciation of his dream. If you ever get a chance to visit Memphis, Tennessee, you must try to reserve a few hours for visiting the National Civil Rights Museum. It is part of the Lorraine Motel on Mulberry Street, the site of the assassination, and it chronicles the struggle for civil rights from the past to the present.

Popcorn Day

January 19

January 19 is National Popcorn Day. We all love the taste of popcorn, especially when we have it at the movie theater. But there are some fun ways to make this day about more than popping a bag into the microwave and heating for a few minutes. Great recipes for a variety of popcorn treats are on the Popcorn Board's website at www.popcorn. org. My favorite is the recipe for cheesy popcorn because I love cheese. Tins of popcorn, available for purchase, that have caramel, cheese, and butter-flavor popcorn are always a hit, if you don't want to go to the trouble of making your own. But making your own popcorn is most of the fun—especially when each child gets to help in the selection and creation of the final product.

According to the Popcorn Board, the first ears of popcorn were found over four thousand years ago. And while I always believed that buttered popcorn tasted better the next day, four thousand-year-old popcorn just doesn't appeal to my taste buds.

According to the Pop Quiz at popcorn.org, "Popcorn pops when the moisture inside the kernel is heated to about 347 degrees and expands to make the delicacy we all love. Popped corn takes up to thirty-seven times more space than unpopped corn. The Popcorn Board's website states that if you covered the state of Oregon with a layer of unpopped kernels, you would have enough popcorn, when popped, to cover the entire United States of America."

So what other fun things can be done with popcorn, besides eating it? We all know about popcorn strings, for decorating a Christmas tree, but I made up a contest to see who could guess the number of kernels, both popped and unpopped, that were inside a jar. I started by having my kids count out the number of unpopped kernels that would fit inside a small glass jar. Then, they had to count the number of popped kernels that fit inside a different, much larger jar. The kids made up a contest to see who in the family could guess the closest to both jars. This game had many benefits. First, it got them to count to numbers that they weren't used to, and, second, it put them in charge of organizing the game and coming up with a small present for the winner. (Sometimes, we parents need to win a prize, too.) Of course, the kids frequently asked for advice on what the prize should be, and I always wanted hugs and kisses equal to the difference of my guess and the correct answer. Shameless on my part, huh? It should come as no surprise that my wife and I purposely guessed a much lesser number than what we really thought it would be. My kids' friends really enjoyed this simple game also, and once they found out the size difference between popped and unpopped corn, they dedicated themselves to finding jars that were proportionally accurate to balance the numbers. It does have a fun effect on adults when they are shown two dramatically different-sized jars, and they need to guess the amounts inside. It comes as a big surprise when the numbers are almost equal.

February

Go Fly a Kite Day

February 8

February 8 is National Kite Flying Day, but the first or second weekend in February is close enough for me, and when you get down to it, a warm, windy day is probably the best kite flying day for your little kids. Any windy day that is not blowing snow is a reason to fly a kite. February is a good month, after all!

Kite flying is such an inexpensive hobby that, for a few dollars, today you can buy and build one in a matter of minutes. That's the source of a great holiday for kids; it provides hours of fun and lets them regale in their pride at being such excellent flyers. They will enjoy learning how to make the kite dip and dive and nosedive and, frankly, will enjoy the serenity of the wind and calmness of the sky.

Besides flying the kite, the most enjoyment my children had was picking out which kite they wanted to use. There are shapes galore, and, of course, they wanted the most complicated, beautiful, and expensive kite ever developed. That was not going to happen, as guess who gets to put them together? Easy is the best way to get started; tell them after they learn how to fly the first few, they can come back and pick out bigger and better ones. Ultimately they chose the most colorful or images of their favorite TV character at the time. I did some research on kites in order to just try and educate the kids on how they were developed. The history is quite fascinating; all I ever knew was the Benjamin Franklin story we were taught in school.

According to Wikipedia, "kites were used approximately twenty-eight hundred years ago in China. The kite was said to be the invention of the famous fifth century BC Chinese philosophers Mozi and Lu Ban. They were used for messages for a rescue mission, measuring distances, testing the wind, lifting men, and communication for military operations. Toward the end of the thirteenth century, Marco Polo returned to Europe with stories of kites. And kites were brought back by sailors from Japan and Malaysia in the sixteenth and seventeenth centuries."

Also, Wikipedia states that, "although they were initially regarded as mere curiosities, by the eighteenth century, kites were being used as vehicles for scientific research." We are still taught that "Benjamin Franklin published a proposal in 1750 for an experiment to prove that lightning is electricity by flying a kite in a storm that appeared capable of becoming a lightning storm." So kites have been around for centuries and continue to provide opportunities for adventure and education.

Wikipedia continues, saying, "The period from 1860 to about 1910 became the "golden age of kiting." Kites started to be used for scientific purposes, especially in meteorology, aeronautics, wireless communications, and photography. World War II saw a limited use of kites for military purposes. Since then they are used mainly for recreation due to a vast improvement in technology."

There are many types of kites, but the most popular are the delta kites, which are shaped like triangles. Other types are called box, flat, bowed, and sled. The jargon used by kite enthusiasts includes: the line (string that you hold), the bridle (loops of string that connect the line to the kite), the reel (what holds the string)—and, trust me, you should always use something other than your hands to hold the string, because it can cut your hands—the leading edge (part of the kite that faces the wind), the trailing edge (the back of the kite), the frame (rods that give it its shape), and the most famous part of the kite, the tail (the part that keeps the kite stable and pointing the right way).

When flying your kite, always watch out for the power lines and run into the wind. Don't be upset if you lose a few kites into the trees or if the kids get a bit discouraged early on as they need to let some string out so the kite can start soaring. But like most things, when they accomplish their first flyer, their faces will be beaming at the accomplishment. When your child flies the kite up into the air for the first time, make sure you record it on film and upload to YouTube!

He or she will love you for it.

Valentine's Day

February 14

We know this is a day to show your love for those special people in your life—usually your spouse or significant other. But let's face it, there is no greater love than what we have for our children. The unconditional nature of parental love, from the moment the child is born, is something only a parent can know and appreciate. And I suspect our significant others would agree.

This is also the most self-indulgent day for me, as you will find. It's all about *kisses*—Hershey's Kisses, in fact. You know, the cute little chocolate candies, which have been an iconic favorite since their introduction in 1907. Kisses got their name from the manufacturing process used to make the teardrop-shaped candies. The machine that made the Kisses also made a sound that echoed the sound of a kiss and—*voilà!*—a legend was born.

As Hershey's began to change the packaging of the candy and introduced wrapping colors other than silver, I began thinking about how I could get what I really wanted from my kids—*more hugs* and *kisses*!

Most parents would agree that kids thrive on structure—ironically, they are stymied by the chaos they often create—and do best in a predictable environment in which they can identify with things that are important to them. Two things they are most comfortable with are their names and ages. Every child knows those two things instinctively and is proud of how those characteristics distinguish him or her from other kids. So let's take a moment and use one of those attributes to make this holiday more fun.

Depending on how many kids you have, pick up packages of Kisses in different colors, one for each child. Silver, gold, red, and purple are just some of the colors available. I used to look around the office, rather than buy packages of the candy, and I would often collect a handful from different coworkers who, around this time of year, always seemed to have their candy dishes filled. Mostly, I think their love of chocolate was masquerading as a celebration of Valentine's Day, but I was okay with that.

Anyway, you will need enough Kisses for your kid's age, plus one, so you can show him or her what to look for. So, if your child is five, you will need six Kisses—five to hide and one to show him or her at the outset. Then, hide those kisses around the house for your child to find. Because the Kisses are so small, it can be fun to see how often the kids miss them, even when they are in plain sight. By the way, never put the Kisses in drawers or in places where something needs to be moved in order to find it. I learned the hard way that doing so just invites havoc and opportunities for destruction. Personally, I like all the candy to be out in the open, although it could be they have to look behind or around something to find their Kiss. I also like to keep it relatively simple and put the treats in just a few rooms or areas, so the kids aren't scavenging over the whole house.

Once they find them all, they give them back to you with a hug and a kiss for each one. (That's the self-indulgent part of this little holiday.) In exchange for the hugs and kisses, I give them a little treat. The younger they are, the more fun it is to give a special ice-cream treat, a trip to Burger King, a little stuffed animal, or just something you know they enjoy. But it should always end with you saying, "I love you." Your children can't hear those words enough, and it helps them bond with you over the years (which you will need as they become teenagers).

As an extra bonus, this little holiday also works wonders for your spouse or significant other. Hide *one* Hershey's Kiss someplace in the house for your spouse to find. It's amazing how quickly we grown-ups revert to childhood and enjoy doing childlike things again. Since your spouse only has to find one, it should be in a difficult spot. Plus, when everyone is looking at the same time, you get some nice peace and quiet, too. The prize for your spouse can be a gift certificate for pampering, dinner out, or, well, you know. This ends the same way—getting a hug and a kiss and saying, "I love you." Of course, who doesn't love a little bit of chocolate, too?

Presidents' Day or "Presents Day" (If You Say It Fast Enough)

The third Monday in February is officially known as Presidents' Day, but originally it was recognized as Washington's birthday, in honor of our first president.

This is a combination holiday. I wanted my kids to understand who all the presidents were, to receive some learning in advance of school, and, generally, to be able to impress adults who have forgotten most of the presidents (except, of course, for those who are pictured on our money).

Anyway, Presidents' Day, or Presents Day, is a holiday in which the kids can earn a small present in exchange for learning about the great leaders of this country.

The education starts with knowing the names of all the presidents, starting with the current one. So, there is memorization, which seems boring, but there are ways to make it fun; and, like many challenging things, this will provide a sense of accomplishment when complete and when you test them at random times and they still remember what they learned. Fortunately, or unfortunately, we moved around a lot, and my kids have resided in several states. Knowing which presidents were born in those states, or what cities in our states were named after presidents, or, in many cities, how streets are named for our presidents is a source of ongoing reinforcement and curiosity. This was not planned as recognition of a president, but my two children are named Zachary and Taylor, who was the twelfth president of the United States, and this was helpful in getting them to learn about the leaders of our nation. Then, we move on to knowing certain characteristics about the presidents.

> Who was the youngest? (John Kennedy)
> Who is on Mount Rushmore? (Washington, Jefferson, Lincoln, Theodore Roosevelt)
> Who was never elected president? (Gerald Ford)
> Who was elected president two times but never reelected? (Grover Cleveland)
> Who was nicknamed Old Rough and Ready? (Zachary Taylor)
> Who were the father/son presidents? (John and John Quincy Adams, plus George H. W. and George W. Bush)
> Who were grandfather/grandson presidents? (William Henry and Benjamin Harrison)
> Who were the presidents that were cousins? (Theodore and Franklin Roosevelt, plus James Madison and Zachary Taylor)
> Who is related to the most presidents? (Franklin Roosevelt—eleven)
> And so many more!

Once they master any level of knowledge you deem appropriate, they may receive their presents. I liked to make the presents tie into the presidents. They will learn quickly who the presidents are on the one-, five-, ten-, and twenty-dollar bill. So, to introduce a little fun into the game, after the kids have completed the process, they can buy something, of their choosing, for the value of one of the bills. You can work this into the form of a game. For instance, each correct answer is worth one dollar. So, the more the child knows, the more he or she can earn. Also, there can be bonus questions worth more money, as well.

For example, one of your questions, for one dollar, might be, "Who was the first president of the United States?" I like to incorporate the kids' ages into the game; so, if a child is seven years old, he or she gets seven questions to answer. The children should always know the president tied to their age, too. For instance, if the child is seven, he or she might like to know that the seventh president was Andrew Jackson. You choose how much money you want to invest. It could be coins, rather than dollars; the choice is yours. The goal is not to give away money, (it could be little pieces of candy) but rather, it is to help them learn. As an added bonus, *you* get to learn a few things, too, because you will be researching the material to quiz them about.

Once they finish the game, obviously praise them for how much they have learned and how smart they are. A child's self-confidence starts with the parent. Children who are praised for their intelligence by their parents will want to keep hearing that praise, and this will help them in school. Education is what can make all the difference in a successful life. It's not the level of school or degree your child achieves; it's the drive to learn that will separate him or her from the rest.

Second, reward them with the value of their bonus money. So, if they correctly answered enough questions to earn ten dollars, give them the ten dollars to spend at the store on whatever they want. It's *their* money, and, with it, you can start teaching them the value of a dollar. You will be amazed at how most kids will really start to appreciate how much things cost in relation to their worth. Usually, the kids start off seeking to buy as many items as possible with the money they have. Later, as they get older, they look to buy one nice thing. Watching your child grow in his or her math skills and impress the checkout clerk is your reward for this game.

Pistachio Nut Day

February 26

Need I say more? I love the white ones; the kids loved the red ones. We would get a bowl of nuts and just sit out in the backyard and eat the nuts and talk about cartoons, or school, or games, or chores. I opened most of the nuts, and they got to enjoy the taste. I would also set up different-sized containers a few feet away from where we were sitting. There was a sand pail, the container the nuts came in, a coffee cup, a drinking glass, and a wide frying pan. After we were done eating, we would have a competition to see who could get the most shells into the containers. It was easy between the red shells and white ones to keep track. From the items listed, they all were different sizes and different levels of difficulty. The frying pan was the largest, but the shells would bounce out. Points were given on a 5-4-3-2-1 basis, and after fifty shells were thrown, the contest was over. They learned that the easiest-looking container (frying pan) was the hardest one, the easiest (sand pail) ultimately got them the most points, and Dad always seemed to lose by just a few points. They were also developing hand-eye coordination that video games cannot replicate.

The winner was the nuttiest of the day! A title they loved to share with Mom and, of course, loved that they beat Dad.

One Day Fun Day

February 29

You may refer to this as a leap day. Although most years in our calendar have 365 days, a complete revolution around the sun takes approximately 365 days *and* six hours. So every four years, an extra twenty-four hours have accumulated, and therefore one extra day is added to keep us coordinated with the sun's position. That's the explanation for the scientists out there.

But for the little (and big) kids out there, since leap day comes along every four years, why not celebrate it? The school may not like this, but the idea here is to take the kids out of school for the day, take the day off from work, and just go have fun together. Visit the zoo, go to the park or the bookstore, have pizza for lunch, and play games together.

Now, those things are pretty easy to do. If you're like me and believe a day that comes once every four years should be a little more special, you could do something a little more extraordinary. Mom could take her daughters for manicures, pedicures, and facials. My daughter loved her One Day Fun Day shopping trip. Dad could take the boys to the arcade, or to play miniature golf. My son loved riding paddle boats on a river. Those are all things that my family didn't normally do, so this One Day Fun Day was of particular enjoyment, especially when we took them out of school and explained that we were taking the day off from work to enjoy being with *them*!

Trust me on this—when you explain to your boss or coworkers why you won't be at work that day, they will be so intrigued and fascinated by the concept that they will tell you how cool you are. Next they'll ask you what other fun things you do with your kids. You already know there are over fifty!

March

Clean Up Your Room Day

March 4

Without a doubt, this is the holiday my kids *hated* most of all. It's the one they remember the most and the one they wish had never come into existence. It is one of the first I invented because March 4, is a little play on words about marching forth and doing something tremendous. Hence, it is Clean Up Your Room Day, because what we wanted the most was getting the rooms cleaned, at least once a year. I have since learned there is a National Clean Up Your Room Day, celebrated on May 10. I didn't know this years ago, and you can celebrate any day you want and use March Forth to get your kids to do other things, such as things at the end of this section, but I am sticking to this date.

Now, many parents have held their kids accountable for keeping their rooms clean, their beds made, and doing some simple chores around the house. We did not set that expectation, and, as a result, we have suffered complete and utter disgust with the current state of affairs in my children's rooms. My daughter, age fourteen, deserves the code name "queen of clutter" because we cannot see the carpet in her room. Instead, we can see all the clothes she owns littered all over the floor.

It doesn't bother her in the slightest. She has friends over for sleepovers and ignores their giggles at how bad her room looks. I don't know if the clothes are clean or dirty. She says they are dirty and just need to be brought downstairs to the laundry room, but I secretly believe that her true objective is to drive her mother insane.

March 4 is about cleaning the rooms your children live in. There is a reward, but they have to really earn it. We're talking about a deep clean here, and not just a little cleaning. One might call this revenge for the year of filth the child has chosen to live in. The bed must be made, and the clothes must be washed and put away. If the clothes end up hidden under the bed or dumped into the closet—which is their first choice—there needs to be a penalty. Make it a good one, because it is actually fun to see the look on your kids' faces when you look under the bed or open the closet door to uncover their true ingenuity and sincere belief at how dumb their parents could be. The first penalty was the vacuuming of the room and the second was the introduction of Windex for the mirrors.

Now, this cleaning takes several hours with the penalty vacuums and Windex and folding methods. Now you know why they hate this day so much as, again, this cleaning takes several hours!

Alas, I cannot declare victory, because there was no success in making the kids maintain their clean rooms for twenty-four hours. In fact, March 5 could be renamed "How Fast Can You Make a Mess Day?" But for one day, we were proud to be the parents of kids with tidy rooms.

The reward at the end of this day is usually a little bigger, in an attempt to recognize the depth of this monumental occasion. Again, depending on their age, a favorite toy or gift card or treat is the satisfaction. Of course, we all might be better off rewarding good behavior on a daily basis, so feel free to throw this holiday away and praise the routine deliverance of tidiness. In fact, simply use this date, March 4, to encourage your kids to do something else entirely, like March Forth and give mom a foot massage, wash the car, give the dog a bath, call Grandma, or just play nicely with their siblings!

Pi(e) Day

March 14

So, it turns out that great minds do think alike. Now, I had thought up Pi(e) Day a long time ago and believed it was my own concoction, but apparently others have the same point of view. In fact, according to wikipedia.com, "Larry Shaw created Pi Day in 1988."

Remember back to high school geometry, when the teacher taught that the ratio of a circle's circumference to its diameter was pi and the formula for determining the area of a circle was pi times r (radius) squared (and we would say, "pie are round")? Well, once you actually do the math and try to solve for pi, which can never be solved, you have the basic foundation that pi=3.14 (approximately, as some computers have the calculation extending into the trillionth place without any repetition of numbers).

Anyway, 3.14, or pi, is most easily recognized on 3/14, or March 14; so it's now known as Pi Day. I changed it to Pie Day, and that is the day we bake pies as a family. Getting the kids involved in the making of a sweet treat is a sweet treat in itself. We first started by purchasing our favorite pies . . . apple, chocolate, and my favorite, lemon meringue. Then, as my wife began to enjoy baking, and as the kids' preferences changed to pecan and pumpkin, we started helping the kids make their favorite pies. I must admit though, as much fun as it was to help the kids with their pies, now that the kids make their pies by themselves, I get to sit back and enjoy what they made with a nice cup of coffee. From this, the kids are learning how to do a project on their own and how to be self-sufficient. And now they can see how simple and gratifying it is to please others with their work efforts.

I also celebrated Pie Day by bringing in a variety of pies for my coworkers once per year, and this has evolved into a great bake-off for the department with homemade pies, secret recipes, and a judging contest for the Pie Maker of the Year!

The one main problem for me has been that eating pies at work and at home, plus leftovers, means I really needed to develop a Daddy Diet Day (or month)!

St. Patrick's Day

March 17

St. Patrick, recognized as the patron saint of Ireland, used the shamrock as a way to promote the holy trinity, the Father, the Son, and the Holy Ghost. According to luckycharmtalisman.com, "the rare four leaf variety, the leaves stand for faith, hope, love, and luck." So, what's green got to do with it? According to Wikipedia, "blue was the original color linked to St. Patrick, but over time, shamrock green became the color associated with St. Patrick's Day. The day is generally when people wear green, and when Lenten restrictions on eating and drinking alcohol are lifted." But this book is not about religion, it's about kids, so how can we have some fun with this?

Drinking green beer is out, but others are in: *Green Eggs and Ham*, by Dr. Seuss, is a must book to read and discuss! Of course, something green must be worn to school, or for the day, by the kids. Participating in the events of this day makes it more fun. How crazy they choose to be is up to them (and you). It's not about forcing green eye shadow, face paint, or socks, but just letting them have fun.

The Internet is actually filled with green treats, recipes, and ideas for fun-filled greenery. Here are some simple foods and activities to enjoy:

> Green scrambled eggs. Add a little green food coloring to your egg mix before cooking in a skillet.
>
> Green omelets. Similar to green scrambled eggs, just add green food coloring to the egg mix and fill the omelet with spinach, green peppers, and some mozzarella cheese.
>
> Green pancakes or waffles. Add a little green food coloring to the batter.
>
> Green milk. Add a *little* food coloring to a glass of milk (stir really well). You can also use green milk in cereal. My kids did not enjoy the green milk and refused to drink. Hopefully they think the same way about green beer many years from now.
>
> Green fruit cups. Cut up green apples, kiwis, grapes, honeydew melon, and pears.
>
> Green cinnamon rolls. Make store-bought cinnamon rolls, but use the green food coloring to change the plain icing color before you frost the rolls.
>
> Go green. This is a perfect time to teach about reducing, reusing, and recycling. I graduated from the University of South Florida, and the school colors are green and gold, so those Bulls T-shirts were extra handy during March.

I also like to hide a few "greenbacks" around the house for the kids to find. In fact, seventeen one-dollar bills nicely braid together the day, the color, and the joy of finding the leprechaun's pot of gold at the end of the rainbow.

Goof-Off Day

March 22

I don't know where this one started, but it quickly became one of my kids' favorites. Put aside all your responsibilities for the day, just chill out, and do what you want—no bed making, no chores, and no homework. (I recommend you clear this with your kids' teachers first. My kids certainly told their teachers that I said they didn't have to do their homework on this day, and guess who got in trouble when the rest of the kids in class said the same thing?)

C'mon, admit it. This is already your favorite holiday and is clearly worth the price of the book! But you have to start preparing your spouse in advance of what you are *not* going to do. And you need to be prepared that the following day, or the day before, will be known as do twice the number of things in a day . . . day.

It's similar to my birthday plan (at the end of the book) of doing whatever you want to do, but you don't have to go anyplace. Supposedly, the number one activity on this day is to play video games. It's hours of mindless fun on any computer, phone, or Xbox, if you have one. According to my wife, this criteria makes it so that every day qualifies as goof-off day for me!

April

April Foolishness

April 1

Sometimes referred to as All Fools' Day, April 1 is widely recognized and celebrated as a day when many people play a variety of pranks on one another. The day is marked by jokes, hoaxes, and other hilarity on friends and family members. Depending on your level of bravery, you might play similar pranks on teachers, neighbors, work associates, or community members such as postal workers, cleaners, etc.

According to Wikipedia,

> In the Middle Ages, New Year's Day was celebrated on March 25 in most European towns. And, in some areas of France, New Year's was a week-long holiday ending on April 1. It is suggested that April Fools' Day originated when those who celebrated on January 1 made fun of those who celebrated on other dates.
>
> Iranians play jokes on each other on the 13th day of the Persian New Year (Norouz), which falls on April 1 or April 2. This day, celebrated as far back as 536 BC, is called Sizdah Bedar and is the oldest prank-tradition in the world still alive today; this fact has led many to believe that April Fools' Day has its origins in this tradition.
>
> In France and French-speaking Canada, the April 1 tradition includes poisson d'avril (literally "April's fish"), attempting to attach a paper fish to the victim's back without being noticed.
>
> In 1539, Flemish poet Eduard de Dene wrote of a nobleman who sent his servants on foolish errands on April 1. In 1686, John Aubrey referred to the holiday as "Fooles

holy day," the first British reference. On April 1, 1698, several people were tricked into going to the Tower of London to "see the Lions washed."

Regardless of where or when the tradition started, this is a classic case of people embracing harmless fun and engaging their imaginations to devise new ways to fool their friends. A few years ago, on April Fools' Day, a retail company I worked for issued a fake press release announcing it had decided to change the color of store-associate uniforms. Another year, the press release cited fake customer research and declared that pennies would no longer be accepted in stores. The press releases formalized the hoaxes, and I remember, the first time I read them, how shocked I was at these new "announcements." Therein lies the beauty of April Foolishness.

Now, how can we incorporate this into our kids' lives?

As a parent, you don't want to humiliate your kids or really embarrass them. Perhaps the proper note to strike is to have some silly fun, which is why I refer to it as April Foolishness Day rather than April Fools' Day. I started by taping notes to their backs that said, "Give me a hug." After a while they would ask, "Why all the hugs?"

I responded by saying, "You asked for it," which they claimed not to have done. That started the discussion and, subsequently, the discovery of the notes on their backs. The key with this holiday is *not* to announce it, but to plant the seed in your child's memory, so that he or she knows, vaguely, that the day is coming. The element of surprise needs to be on your side.

I also liked to ask the kids to tell four jokes they knew, or learned for this. I asked for one joke for each member of our family, and each joke had to be tailored for dad, mom, brother, or sister. I also asked them to tell one joke that made the teller of the joke laugh.

As they got older, I encouraged them to try similar things with us, their parents, so we could all have fun and laugh at ourselves. You will, of course, have to know what they are doing, but play along anyway.

The hoaxes became a little more elaborate as the circumstances of the household changed. One time, my daughter needed to get ready for a party, and when she went to take her usual shower, I turned off the water to the house. She was in a literal panic, because her hair was "disgusting," and she worried she was going to miss the party because we didn't have water in the house. It was hilarious. I picked up that bit of humor from a neighbor, who told me that he had had a party at his house on New Year's Eve in 1999, when all the concern was whether all computers would shut down because of something everyone called the Y2K bug. He went to the basement and, at midnight, tripped the main breaker of the house and turned off all the electricity. His wife wondered aloud, as part of the hoax, if the Y2K bug was the problem. The revelers had a good discussion, in the dark, until one partier saw other homes had electricity. Every year, they talk about that New Year's Eve hoax.

This is a day of harmless pranks, so you might consider some of the following pranks (attempt at your own risk!):

Putting sugar in the salt shaker

Switching some of the keys around on the computer keyboard

Unscrewing the light bulbs in the prankee's room

While the prankee is sleeping, placing a few red dots on his or her face

Placing a call to your home answering machine and announcing that you are part of a survey crew calling to say that the driveway is not on your property anymore, and you must get a zoning variance

Turning off the wireless switch on the laptop, resulting in a lost Internet connection

Replacing good milk with spoiled for morning cereal

Moving the toaster setting to the highest level and burning the toast (make sure there's enough bread to replace it)

And, my favorite, tuning the radio stations in the car to all Spanish programming

One time, I got home early and "stole" certain things from the house. I moved the TV set, the iPod, the laptop, and a couple of paintings. I emptied the kids' piggy banks and messed up their drawers, and then I left to do some shopping. When I returned, everyone thought we had been robbed. *That* was a good one. All the loot was in the basement!

My wife likes to keep her same eyeglasses frames and just replace the lenses when her vision changes. So, I kept the old lenses for a year, and then, the night before April Fools' Day, I replaced her new lenses with the old ones. Her eyesight got worse that morning!

Of course, your kids (and spouse) will learn to retaliate and embrace the meaning of the holiday too. So, watch your back! I woke up one morning with my fingernails painted. I also got the "punch me" yellow Post-it note on my back and figured it out after a few little fist bumps unexpectedly met my arm.

At one point, I learned to stop buying socks that were unique, so that I didn't have to spend time sorting them to get a matched set. Instead, I bought many pairs of the same-style sock, so they all matched. They were all black, too. My kids bought some blue ones, though, and mismatched them in my drawer. When I put them on in the morning, I wore one black sock and one blue sock to work that day. Excellent!

They also redid some of my piano music notes. I can't play the notes from just reading the sheet music. Rather, I need to write the actual chord letters on the paper. My kids made some up, and they erased some of my notes. Then, they replaced them in my music holder, and I would mess those pieces up completely. They would then yell "April Fools'!" sometimes months later.

Having a sense of humor is so important. Teaching boundaries at some point is also critical to do, in advance. Hiding my car keys when I was running late for work was a strain on my sense of humor. They learned that a little fun was okay at each other's expense, but when human emotions came into play, it was time to stop. I hope that is a good life lesson, too.

Easter

Easter is celebrated on the first Sunday following the first full moon after the spring equinox. This usually occurs on March 21, which means Easter can fall anytime between March 22 and April 25 depending on the lunar cycle. Most of the time, it falls in April. I prefer to look at a new calendar to find out when it is. Having worked in the retail industry for many years, Easter is a time when increased sales can move from one month to the next. Retail analysts have even have coined terms such as "Mapril" or "Marpril" to combine the two months together, as a means of determining how sales were in the Easter season.

Now, as you may have gathered, I will not be talking about Easter in a religious context. Rather, I'll focus on the enjoyment of kids celebrating Easter in the traditional way, with the Easter bunny and Easter eggs.

While Valentine's Day may be gaining traction, Easter is the first *big*, commercial holiday of the calendar year, with abundant marketing of candy, Easter baskets, greeting cards, songs, and, of course, Peter Cottontail. Every businessman in America seems to be cashing in on this one, and I am no different. My enthusiasm for Easter is attributable to my love of hard-boiled eggs. I don't like the yolk, but peeling off the shell and eating the white with a little salt makes me feel "egg-static."

This holiday starts with eggs and ends with lottery tickets. (You'll see what I mean as you read on.)

Let's get started. First, we have to hard-boil the eggs. I know this is a complicated chore and often results in overcooking, but, to me, the perfect hard-boiled egg can be peeled in about twenty seconds. That's when the shell comes off in big pieces. Here is my formula:

- Lay your eggs on the bottom of the pot, without stacking them on top of each other
- Fill the pot with water to cover at least one inch over the eggs
- Put on high heat, and bring to a rapid boil for about twelve minutes
- Remove the eggs immediately from the pot, and plunge them into cold water until you can pick them out of the water without burning your hands
- Let them dry and cool in the refrigerator

Then, it's time to decorate them; PAAS Easter Egg Dye to the rescue! This venerable Easter egg dyeing company seems to exist for one purpose, which is to color eggs. (The name comes from Pasen, the Pennsylvania Dutch name for Easter.) But they have taken up their cause and run with it! The variety of egg-dye packages is really something to behold. While you're decorating eggs, you might have to snack on Peeps candy. Peeps Marshmallow candy started in the 1950s and, according to wikianswers.com, is "the second most popular candy during Easter" (chocolate bunnies are first, of course . . . mainly the ears!)

So, once you have your Easter egg dyeing kit from the store, just follow the simple instructions to set up your egg-dyeing station. Before you dip the eggs in the dye, though, use a crayon and write one letter of each of your kids' names on the shells of the eggs that you're decorating. Go over the letters twice, and they will appear white after the dyeing is done. The wax from the crayon seals the eggshell dry, which means the dye won't absorb on that part of the egg.

After you dye the eggs and let them dry, you will have colored eggs—which spell out your children's names—that are ready to be hidden. And who does the hiding? Well, the Easter Bunny, of course! He comes and hides a basket of candy- or coin-filled plastic eggs along with hard-boiled eggs, because he knows how much Dad loves hard-boiled eggs. It would be great if the Easter Bunny left a map indicating where he hid the eggs, because it always seems that a few of his plastic eggs are never found.

Obviously, your children need to find all the eggs so that they may spell out their names. Once they do that and turn those in to Dad, they get one present. Personally, I liked the big Easter baskets at Wal-Mart or Kmart, or big, stuffed Easter Bunnies for their rooms. Again, this holiday is not so much about the present as it is about the egg hunt and building your Easter traditions together. Again, any religious education or tradition will be up to you to incorporate.

Now that the eggs have been found, you can add more "egg-citement" to your holiday. Do you know that, when you tap two hard-boiled eggs together, only one of the shells will break? Well, choose your egg wisely, grasshopper; everyone gets to play in this game. Think of it as an eggy March Madness, with brackets up against each other. The egg that survives the tapping will be the winner. This entitles the chooser of that egg to get a special prize.

I hate to admit it, but my kids really like scratching off lottery tickets. So, here are the choices I have been giving them recently. The winner gets to choose ten one-dollar lottery tickets, five two-dollar tickets, or five dollars in cash. They receive the winnings on the tickets, too, if there are any. This may not be your cup of tea, of course, in which case a special dessert or game can be the "egg-stra" prize. The other kids get the leftover lottery tickets, as consolation prizes. The winning egg should also be the first egg to be eaten, as it's always the best tasting. We "ooh" and "ahh" over how good it is, as well as praising the child who picked it out!

Cloud Day

April 12

Another simple, no-cost holiday is to enjoy a spring day just sitting with your kids in your backyard, looking up into the sky and letting your imagination run wild to see how many shapes of animals and other things you can identify in the clouds. Your kids will impress you with the way their minds work, and everyone will enjoy the fun. How many ducks, hot dogs, swans, faces, and flags can you come up with? Of course, if you want this also to be a teaching moment, talk to your kids about what clouds are and teach them those crazy names, such as:

> Stratus (the low clouds that are thin, gray, and sheet-like)
> Altostratus (the middle clouds that are grayish and hide the sun)
> Cirrus (the high clouds that are thin and feather-like)
> Cirrocumulus (the high clouds that are like cotton patches)
> Cumulus (the vertical clouds that are fair weather, with flat bases and dome-shaped tops)
> Altocumulus (the patchy solid clouds with rounded shapes)
> Nimbus (the precipitation clouds)
> And when you put nimbus with cumulus, you get the vertical clouds with bulging tops that bring thunder, lightning, and showers.

Your kids will have a step up on all the other kids in earth science!

Clouds are not the only things that your imagination can redefine into other objects. I recently went on a trip to Antarctica, and it amazed me that I could look at all the ice chunks floating in the water and see similar shapes as when I look at clouds. I saw swans with long necks, hot dogs, flying ducks, snakes, and trees, and some of the ice floes were bigger than ships. Obviously none of them produced any precipitation other than melting, but the sun certainly reflected beautifully off their shapes. Whether the sky or the water, nature has managed to produce an amazing array of shapes to inspire the mind.

Juggler's Day

April 18

Once you learn to juggle, you will amaze your friends by juggling anything. I was around eighteen when I learned to juggle. As I was suntanning myself in a Florida backyard, I noticed there was an orange tree in bloom, and, out of boredom, I taught myself how to juggle oranges. After a few hours of practice, I have never forgotten.

Here are the simple steps:

> Place two balls in your right hand, and one in your left
> Toss one ball from your right hand upward at a slight angle around left ear height
> Just before you catch the first ball, toss the ball you are holding in your left hand upward at a slight angle to your right ear height
> Just before that ball lands, toss the ball in your right hand up and repeat the steps

If you are left-handed, just do the opposite as above.

With this method, you will have one ball in each hand and one continually in the air. There are many other types of juggling you can do, but, really, juggling three balls is the classic style. For my kids, golf balls were the easiest for their small hands to catch. *Be outside* when you practice. The kids did like to try rocks, and I tried other objects, such as a golf ball, a tennis ball, and an apple, all at once, and once you can do different items, juggling is always available to amaze other kids.

Juggling is one of those things everyone wants to do, but most don't spend the time it takes to practice.

When your kids master the technique and show off their skills to other kids, they will love it, especially for boys when they're old enough to impress the girls!

Jelly Bean Day

April 22

According to squidoo.com,

> No one really knows where jelly beans came from. Many believe that they are descendants of Turkish Delight, which have been around since at least the mid 1800s.
>
> The modern version of these sweet treats made their appearance during the American Civil War when William Schrafft of Boston wanted people to send candy to the soldiers who were in the Union Army.
>
> Jelly beans began to be more of an Easter Candy in the 1930s because they look like mini Easter eggs. Since then many companies have begun to create different sizes as well as yummy flavors of jelly beans. Now you can find them in almost any flavor. Most of the flavored beans come from the Jelly Belly Corporation, however many companies do make them in a variety of flavors.

I hid these little treats around the house, with one color for each child and one per letter of their first name. So, for instance, I would hide six red jelly beans for Taylor and seven green jelly beans for Zachary. Once they found their colors, they could have an additional twenty-two total jelly beans, one for each day of the month leading up to Jelly Bean Day. A variation is hiding twenty-two jelly beans, or one for every birthday they have had.

We learned, after we got a little puppy, that the dog could find the jelly beans much faster than my kids could. Then there was the jelly bean mess day.

Each of the kids had a favorite jelly bean flavor, and half the fun seemed to be trying out new ones. My dad always preferred the black ones, and I admit I have a fondness for those, but nowadays the smaller ones are more flavorful to me. To me, candy dishes were made for bright, cheap, and cheerful treats such as Skittles, jelly beans, and M&Ms.

May

May Day Play Day

Generally, the first weekend of the month is when I like to play with this one. It's usually warm outside, and it's a good time to give the kids some control over what they do. As you have probably figured out by now, I enjoy creating a treasure hunt atmosphere for the kids to have to work to find things. May Day Play Day is no exception. This was a way for all of us to bond by doing these activities together.

May Day Play Day starts with my favorite number, three. So, for example, I hide three balls around the house. When found, they represent the following three activities for the day:

> The first ball represents the kids' favorite foods.
> The second ball stands for their favorite toys.
> The third ball is for their favorite things to do as a family.

The key to remember is that the kids get to decide what happens. If you have more than one child, you may have to ask all the kids to compromise on what the family does together. That gives them a great start in learning good communication skills and seeing how the balance of power can shift. To avoid too many conflicts, you may have to have a few things ready for their consideration.

I generally buy the toys for them or put a price limit on what they may choose. When they were younger, Chuck E. Cheese's was usually on the docket for favorite food—pizza, of course—and favorite thing to do, which was play in the arcade. This was pretty convenient until my daughter figured out she could partner with her brother and split things up for lunch and dinner and eat at two great places rather than one. Since I love fast food, having lunch at Chuck E. Cheese's and dinner at McDonald's was okay with me. The kids certainly loved it, too.

For things to do, I often suggest different things based on the weather and/or pricing options. A movie, a AAA baseball game, or a game of bowling were all things they wanted to do as a family. I also had a general rule that we needed to be done by 6:00 p.m., as the daylight can stretch pretty long on May Day Play Day.

Now, as the kids are getting older, I still hide three items, but the items hidden got smaller as the kids got smarter. The kids still always won, which was the point.

Mother's Day

Mother's Day is an annual holiday that recognizes mothers, as well the positive contributions that they make to society. In the United States it is celebrated on the second Sunday in May. In its present form, according to Wikipedia,

> Mother's Day was established by Anna Jarvis following the death of her mother Ann Jarvis on May 9, 1905, with the help of Philadelphia merchant John Wanamaker. A small service was held on May 12, 1907, in the Andrew's Methodist Episcopal Church in Grafton, West Virginia where Anna's mother had been teaching Sunday school . . . She then campaigned to establish Mother's Day first as a U.S. national holiday and then later as an international holiday.
>
> The holiday was declared officially by the state of West Virginia in 1910, and the rest of states followed quickly. On May 8, 1914, the U.S. Congress passed a law designating the second Sunday in May as Mother's Day and then on May 9, 1914, President Woodrow Wilson issued a proclamation declaring the first national Mother's Day as a day for American citizens to show the flag in honor of those mothers whose sons had died in war.

This book has focused on holidays that have been designed for the enjoyment of the kids. Mother's Day and Father's Day are occasions when the tables are turned, and the children can show off their abilities to make these two days special for their parents. I read someplace that the letters in "family" could be seen as an acronym representing the following: Father And Mother I Love You

I always thought, *what is the best way to show Mom how much she means?* Pictures and words on their own are the best; they are the most touching way to show your mom you care. Ask your kids to list reasons why they love having their mom. Ask each child to list one reason for every year of his or her life. The list starts with "I love my mom because . . ."

Mom will cherish those lists forever, or most of them will. You could do the same thing for Father's Day. Hugs and kisses mean a lot, but words, drawings, and pictures will last forever. They are items that never get thrown away by parents.

I have to admit, I have fallen into that common trap of not doing much for my wife on Mother's Day, while uttering those infamous words, "You are not my mother." Be careful; the calendar is a cruel joke for dads in that Mother's Day is strategically positioned before Father's Day. And moms remember everything! "You are not my father," was repeated back to me every time I opened my mouth on Mother's Day. And as you will read in the June chapter, Americans' acceptance of Father's Day was much harder to come by, whereas Mother's Day was embraced almost immediately.

If you really want to score points with your spouse, use the same formula and list reasons why your spouse is such a good mother.

Memorial Day

Memorial Day is observed on the last Monday of May. Formerly known as Decoration Day, it commemorates US soldiers who died while serving in the military.

This holiday is for kids to know that people have helped make this a great country and that many have given their lives so we can enjoy so many things, such as the holidays in this book.

We have bought many small flags and placed them around our sidewalks, to show a simple tribute to these wonderful men and women. The kids put them in the ground and pick them up the next day. The same tribute is paid during Veterans Day.

This is also the traditional beginning of summer. In two of our previous homes, we were fortunate enough to have swimming pools. The kids enjoyed launching the rafts into the pool. Despite the water temperature being a bit too cold for me, we jumped in and got summer started. For the houses where we didn't have built-in pools, a trip to Target and the purchase of an inflatable pool helped to bridge our tradition. The size was enough to accommodate us as we stretched out, and we could control the temperature by filling it with warm water from the faucet.

We also mark this time as the official start of the grilling season, when each kid chooses one item to be grilled. Fortunately, hamburgers and hot dogs are always preferred. My wife, of course, wants asparagus, or slow-cooked ribs, which is her way of getting me out of the house for most of the day.

When the kids were younger, there was also a little test about Memorial Day. I would question them on some battles the United States was involved in, and, in particular, I would ask about some of the US generals of those battles such as:

> The Revolutionary War: George Washington
> The War of 1812: Andrew Jackson
> Mexican-American War: Zachary Taylor
> The Civil War: Ulysses S. Grant, Robert E. Lee
> World War I: John Pershing
> World War II George Patton, Douglas MacArthur, Dwight D.
>   Eisenhower, and Chester Nimitz

If you really want to see how all the games from all the different holidays come together, then ask your kids which president was in office during a specific time frame. They also start to see how many presidents were elected because they were good soldiers.

It's a little test, but, again, the point is to observe the memory of those who gave their lives so we could have the freedoms we cherish today and the ability to enjoy a pool, or a grill, or a day off from school.

Hamburger Day

May 28

Isn't every day a chance to eat a hamburger? It may even coincide with Memorial Day for two holidays in one. According to gone-ta-pott. com, "National Hamburger Day is a bit confusing when it comes to the date. We found references that claimed December 21, July 28, and May 29 as National Hamburger Day.

It is possible that there's more than one Hamburger Day but it must be noted that the date mostly publicized in radio and news media is May 28th!" Whichever one you choose, it is really the most deserving food holiday, although Pizza Day is a close second (see November) in my mind.

So what is so special about hamburgers? According to About.com and the Iowa Beef Industry Council, "The hamburger is America's favorite sandwich with 86 percent of the population ordering them last year."

How did the hamburger get its name? According to the Iowa Beef Industry Council, the answer lies in the following three statements:

> "From the Baltic provinces of Russia in the Middle Ages where rowdy, nomadic tribes of Tartary developed a fondness for raw beef, known today as steak Tartar.
>
> "From the German trading partners of the Tartars who lived in Hamburg; they developed a taste for raw beef fried with onions, called Hamburg Steak.
>
> "From German immigrants who brought "Hamburg Steak" to the US in the 1700s and 1800s."

The Council further states, "In 1888, an English doctor named Salisbury prescribed three hamburger meals a day as a cure for various ailments and is remembered today as the name of a seasoned ground beef patty served with gravy."

Finally, "Almost one thousand quarter-pound hamburgers come from the ground beef of a one thousand-pound steer." There are many more fun facts to check out on hamburgers when you are ready.

My wife's favorite hamburger is a barbeque bacon cheeseburger, while my daughter just likes her hamburgers plain, and I like the basic mustard, ketchup, lettuce, and pickles version. Salt and pepper to taste.

And if you never heard it before, enjoy Jimmy Buffet's hit song "Cheeseburger in Paradise"!

So, pull out the grill and sizzle up a few of your favorites for a nice, entertaining meal.

June

Opposite Day

June 9

This day is simply about changing the normal routine—thinking outside the box and taking nothing for granted. This day has a sister day, which is September 6, when the numbers six and nine are both inverted. I have heard about these opposite days before, but I just came up with things to do on our own. You can take Opposite Day to any level you like, but, for us, the most common activities included:

> A breakfast of hamburgers and hot dogs
> Only dessert for lunch, of the kids' choosing
> Breakfast for dinner—toast, pancakes, scrambled eggs

Depending on how dedicated you want to be, it might help you to know that we sometimes did the following "opposite" things:

> Kids decide when the parents go to bed.
> Kids do the laundry, take out the trash, and/or clean the toilets, etc., while parents play games.
> Kids pick the TV shows or use the computer first.
> The family stays in pajamas all day long.
> Nobody has to brush teeth unless he or she wants to.
> Kids tuck their parents into bed and read them a bedtime story.
> The dishes can stay on the table after eating.
> Opposite Day is a good change of pace once in a while, and my kids always enjoyed being the "parents." I admit it was humbling to hear our own words thrown right back at us

about what we weren't doing right, and I always enjoyed asking them for money so I could go see a movie.

When we switched foods, though, that really caused them some angst. Anything other than cereal or toast in the morning was just wrong! In all, it was a fun way to try new things and get the kids to function outside the typical routine.

Father's Day

Father's Day is a widely known celebration honoring fathers and their influence in society. It is celebrated on the third Sunday in June.

According to royalgazette.com, "It took many years to make the holiday official. In spite of support from many sources, including churches, the YMCA and YWCA, Father's Day ran the risk of disappearing from the calendar. While Mother's Day was met with enthusiasm, Father's Day was often met with laughter."

According to Wikipedia,

> A bill to accord national recognition of the holiday was introduced in Congress in 1913. In 1916, President Woodrow Wilson wanted to make it official, but Congress resisted, fearing that it would become commercialized. US President Calvin Coolidge recommended in 1924 that the day be observed by the nation, but stopped short of issuing a national proclamation. Two earlier attempts to formally recognize the holiday had been defeated by Congress. In 1957, Maine Senator Margaret Chase Smith wrote a proposal accusing Congress of ignoring fathers for forty years while honoring mothers, thus "[singling] out just one of our two parents." In 1966, President Lyndon B. Johnson issued the first presidential proclamation honoring fathers, designating the third Sunday in June as Father's Day. Six years later, the day was made a permanent national holiday when President Richard Nixon signed it into law in 1972.

So, for a day it took so long to recognize, how does our nation really honor its fathers? According to wikipedia.com, "While Mother's Day has the highest number of phone calls, the most collect calls are made on Father's Day." That hardly seems fair. "Hi, Mom!" is a favorite saying among athletes on TV. Where is, "Hi, Dad"? Part of this book is to help give dads an opportunity to be a bigger part of their children's life. It did for me. For Father's Day, ask your kids to list reasons why they love having you as their dad. As they did for Mother's Day, have them try to write one reason for every year of their lives. And if you are married, your spouse can now return the favor as to why her husband is such a great dad. You will cherish those lists forever, or most of them.

Ice-Cream Soda Day

June 20

A simple day at the ice-cream parlor in June is all you need to commemorate this holiday. Be forewarned, the kids want this to be every day in June!

Toothbrush Day

June 26

How appropriate is it that, shortly after Ice-Cream Soda Day, is Toothbrush Day? Well, the toothbrush was invented in 1498, and I always used this day to give the kids a brand-new toothbrush, as well as review how I thought the tooth fairy worked (when they were younger).

I told the kids that June 26 was the tooth fairy's least favorite day because she collected more teeth before the toothbrush was invented. So, if a child lost a tooth on that day, the tooth fairy would bring double her normal donation. After a few moments where the kids really tried pulling them out before they were ready to come out, I found out the tooth fairy had changed her thinking because the teeth were so much cleaner after the toothbrush was invented that she now doubled the donation on *all* the kids' teeth.

It was always a mystery why the tooth fairy had different levels of payment for lost teeth. For my kids, she brought a gold dollar coin for their eye teeth because those were the most valuable. She brought regular dollars for the rest of the teeth. Now, we never found out what she did with all those teeth, but I told the children that I thought she was building a beautiful, shiny white home, and, because teeth were made of enamel, the hardest substance in the body, that house would last forever!

July

Independence Day

July 4

This holiday, of course, celebrates our nation's declaration of independence. "It is commonly associated with fireworks, parades, barbeques, carnivals, fairs, picnics, concerts, baseball games, family reunions, (. . .) and various other public and private events celebrating the history, government, and traditions of the United States," according to wikipedia.com. For kids, July 4th is all about fireworks and barbeques. The fireworks celebration can be tiring, as it usually starts around 9:00 p.m. and usually lasts thirty minutes. It is something you usually have to drive to, and from, and it can be taxing on parents. Once you make up your mind to do it, you'll learn how much fun it is. As you can probably guess, I liked to do a little research on fireworks shows first.

According to Wikipedia, "the Chinese made the first fireworks in the 800s to scare away evil spirits at the New Year." According to tradition, Marco Polo brought the Chinese technology back to Europe.

As outlined in squidoo.com and life123.com, some traditional names of fireworks that can be purchased are:

> **Firecrackers:** The classics, these often come in strips and can be lit with one fuse. They are best known for the amount of noise they can create.
> **Fountains:** These create sparks that flow up like fountains and spill on the ground.
> **M-80s and Cherry Bombs:** You may come across these fireworks in your search, but leave them alone, even if the seller swears up and down they are legal. These are actually illegal because they pack so much power.

Pinwheels: These feature sticks driven into the ground, with the firework spinning at the top of the stick.

Repeaters (aka Cakes): These are small tubes packed together. They can be lit by one fuse, which means you get a big show for minimal effort.

Rockets: As the name indicates, these launch into the air and then explode.

Roman Candles and Tubes: These fireworks launch from a tube and go high into the air.

Shells: Like rockets, these are fired into the air, but then they burst open in a pattern.

Snaps: These small firecrackers are thrown and make a snapping sound. Kids like these, though they shouldn't be allowed to throw them at each other and should be kept away from young kids, who might put them in their mouths.

Sparklers: These fireworks can be held by a stick, and they set off sparks. These seem as safe as snaps, but children can hold them too close, and the sparks might catch their clothing on fire. Kids love sparklers, but adults should be the ones holding them. If you are a sparkler fan, hold it away from your body.

You may check out some of the big firework shows online to see all the great types of professional fireworks. More names of fireworks include: Chrysanthemums, Roman Candles, Poinsettias, Rings, Palm, Wagon Wheel, Dahlia, Crackles, Fountains, Phoenix, Waterfalls, Shells, Brocade, Strobes, Coconuts, Peony, and Croisettes.

I liked to have the kids draw them in crayon, showing how the fireworks open up, and then label them. This may seem like a lot of effort, but when your kids are in a crowd, and they can correctly name the fireworks they are seeing, the people around them will be in awe of how smart your kids really are.

My advice is to take your children to a show and only let them use a simple sparkler back at home. Do-it-yourself fireworks shows cause up to five thousand injuries per year. I'd rather put up with a little inconvenience and listen to the ooohs and ahhs of the audience than see anyone hurt.

Learn about the fifty states as we celebrate our history

Besides just watching fireworks, I wanted my kids to have an appreciation for all the states in our union, particularly because we have visited many as a family, and I have been to all fifty. The kids have counted the ones they have visited, and they were both marvels in school because of some things they learned about the states and their capitals. Thanks to www.50states.com and www.factmonster.com, I was able to accumulate many of the details listed below.

State	Entry Into United State	Year of States Entry	Capitol	Interesting Facts
Alabama	22	1819	Montgomery	The only state with all natural resources to make iron and steel. Introduced Mardi Gras to the Western world. Built the first rocket capable of putting humans on the moon.
Alaska	49	1959	Juneau	The only state that doesn't collect state sales or personal income tax. Purchased for two cents per acre from Russia. The largest of all the states.
Arizona	48	1912	Phoenix	Home to Grand Canyon National Park The number one copper producing state. The only state that has an English-only law in public school.
Arkansas	25	1836	Little Rock	The only state where diamonds have been mined.

				Wal-Mart Corp. opened its first store in Bentonville Pine Bluff is world's center for archery bow production.
California	31	1860	Sacramento	The state with most major league baseball teams (five). More turkeys are raised here than any other state. The first motion picture theater opened here in 1902.
Colorado	38	1876	Denver	The only state to reject offer to host the Olympics. The US Air Force Academy is in Colorado Springs. Denver lays claim to invention of the cheeseburger.
Connecticut	5	1788	Hartford	The first telephone book was published here and listed fifty names. Cattle branding started here when farmers were required to mark their pigs. Home to the first hamburger, Polaroid camera, helicopter, and color TV.
Delaware	1	1787	Dover	The first state to ratify the Constitution. The only state without a national park. The first state to fly Betsy Ross's American flag.
Florida	27	1846	Tallahassee	Saint Augustine is the oldest European settlement in North America. Gatorade was named for the University of Florida, home of the Gators, where it was developed.

Key West has highest average temperature in the United States.

| Georgia | 4 | 1788 | Atlanta | The chicken capital of the world is in Gainesville. Home of the Okeefenokee Swamp. Coca-Cola was invented in Atlanta. |

| Hawaii | 50 | 1959 | Honolulu | The only state that was once a kingdom with its own monarchy. The only state that grows coffee. The widest state in the United States. |

| Idaho | 43 | 1890 | Boise | Has the longest Main Street in America. Hell's Canyon is the deepest gorge in America. Only state without a veterans' cemetery. |

| Illinois | 21 | 1818 | Springfield | Home of Sears Tower, the tallest building in the United States. The world's first skyscraper was built here in 1885. The ice-cream "sundae" was named here. |

| Indiana | 19 | 1816 | Indianapolis | The first long distance auto race was held in 1911. Where Lewis and Clark started their exploration of the Northwest Territory. The Raggedy Ann doll was created here in 1914. |

Iowa	29	1846	Des Moines	The only state bordered entirely by rivers on two sides. The shortest and steepest railroad in the United States. The home of the world's largest strawberry.
Kansas	34	1861	Topeka	Helium discovered here in 1905. Dodge City is the windiest city in the United States. Home of geographic center of the 48 contiguous United States.
Kentucky	15	1774	Frankfort	The Kentucky Derby is the oldest continuous sporting event in the United States. Has the longest underground cave in the world at three hundred miles. Has the only waterfall in the world with a moonbow, which is a rainbow at night.
Louisiana	18	1812	Baton Rouge	The only state without counties—they aere called parishes instead. Has the world's longest bridge over water in the world in Metairie. In 1803, the United States paid France $15 million for the Louisiana Purchase, which nearly doubled our size.
Maine	23	1820	Augusta	The only state that shares a border with just one other state. The eastern-most part of the United States.

The only state whose name is one syllable.

Maryland	7	1788	Annapolis	The only state where judges wear red robes. Home to the United States Naval Academy in Annapolis. The national anthem was created here.
Massachusetts	6	1788	Boston	The first World Series was held here. The first subway system originated here. Fig Newtons were named for the city of Newton.
Michigan	26	1837	Lansing	The University of Michigan was the first university established by the states. Home to the car capital of the world in Detroit and the cereal capital of the United States in Battle Creek. The only state that touches four of the Great Lakes.
Minnesota	32	1858	Saint Paul	Has the oldest rock in the world at 3.8 billion years old. The stapler was invented here. The Better Business Bureau was founded here.
Mississippi	20	1817	Jackson	Elvis Presley was born here. Home to the International Checkers Hall of Fame. Root beer was invented here.
Missouri	24	1821	Jefferson City	Had the most powerful earthquake in the United States.

				Other than Rome, Kansas City has more fountains than any other city in the world. Named for Missouri Indians; name means town of the large canoes.
Montana	41	1889	Helena	Home to Virginia City, the most complete original town in the United States. Home to the largest migratory elk herd in the United States. Known for the highest grizzly bear population in lower 48 states.
Nebraska	37	1867	Lincoln	The only roller skating museum in the world. The birthplace of the Rueben sandwich. More miles of rivers than any other state.
Nevada	36	1864	Carson City	The slot machine was invented here. The largest gold-producing state. *Nevada* is Spanish for snow-clad.
New Hampshire	9	1788	Concord	The first potato planted in the United States. The first free public library was opened here. The only state that does not require public schools to offer kindergarten.
New Jersey	3	1787	Trenton	The car theft capital of the world. Has the highest population density.

World's first drive-in movie theater was built here.

State				
New Mexico	47	1912	Santa Fe	Smokey the Bear was named here. Has the highest capital city, at seven thousand feet above sea level. Home of the Navajo, the largest Native American group.
New York	11	1788	Albany	Fashion Institute of Technology is the only school in the world offering a degree in cosmetics. The first presidential inauguration was held here. Home to the oldest running newspaper, the *New York Post*.
North Carolina	12	1789	Raleigh	The first English child was born here in 1587. The furniture capital of the world is in High Point. The first successful powered air flight was in Kitty Hawk, by the Wright Brothers.
North Dakota	39	1889	Bismarck	The geographic center of North America. Milk is the official state beverage. *Dakota* is a Native American word for friend.
Ohio	17	1803	Columbus	Home of the Rock-and-Roll and Pro Football Halls of Fame, in Cleveland and Canton, respectively. The only state flag shaped like a pennant.

				The first city to use police cars, in Akron.
Oklahoma	46	1907	Oklahoma City	The first city to install a parking meter. The first shopping cart was invented here. Home to National Cowboy Hall of Fame, in Oklahoma City.
Oregon	33	1859	Salem	Has more ghost towns than any other state. Crater Lake is the deepest lake in the United States. Has the only state flag with different pictures on each side.
Pennsylvania	2	1787	Harrisburg	The first magazine was published here. Second state to sign the Declaration of Independence, after Delaware. The chocolate capital of the United States, thanks to the Hershey's Company.
Rhode Island	13	1790	Providence	The smallest state in the United States. The home of the first circus. Home to oldest schoolhouse in the United States, in Portsmouth.
South Carolina	8	1788	Columbia	The first tea farm in the United States. The peach capitol of the world, in Johnston. The first battle of the Civil War took place at Fort Sumter.

South Dakota	40	1889	Pierre	The home of Mount Rushmore, which took fourteen years to complete. Will have the world's tallest sculpture, in Crazy Horse. The geographic center of *all* the fifty United States.
Tennessee	16	1796	Nashville	The birthplace of country music, in Bristol. The home of the National Civil Rights Museum, in Memphis. The second-most-visited house in the United States is Elvis Presley's Graceland.
Texas	28	1845	Austin	The only state to have flags of six different nations fly over the capital. The place where Dr Pepper was invented. Produces more wool than any other state.
Utah	45	1847	Salt Lake City	Had the nation's first department store. Has the largest natural stone bridge in the world, called Rainbow Bridge. Houses the completion point of the first intercontinental railroad.
Vermont	14	1791	Montpelier	The only state capital without a McDonald's. Home of the Ben and Jerry's ice-cream factory. Largest producer of maple syrup in the United States.
Virginia	10	1788	Richmond	The birthplace of our nation—Jamestown was the first English settlement.

				Celebrated the first Thanksgiving in America, in 1619. Kentucky and West Virginia were formed from sections of Virginia.
Washington	42	1889	Olympia	The only state named for a United States president. The only state to have both deserts and rain forests. Produces more apples than any other state.
West Virginia	35	1863	Charleston	Mother's Day was first observed here. The first state to have a sales tax. Considered the southernmost northern state and northernmost southern state.
Wisconsin	30	1848	Madison	The typewriter was invented here. Produced more dairy products than any other state. Home to the Hamburger Hall of Fame.
Wyoming	44	1890	Cheyenne	The first state to give women the right to vote. Has the lowest population in the United States. Home to Yellowstone National Park, the first national park in the United States.

There are many more interesting things, but I tried to pick items that were interesting to the children and that made for entertaining discussions in the car. I encouraged the kids to learn a little more about the state we were living in when this holiday rolled around. In particular, it was fun to learn the origins of the name of the state and city where we lived. Usually, the names had roots in Native American names, and it's amazing how few of us know the history about where we live. This holiday can be for everyone to learn something new!

Macaroni Day

July 7

This is the day to enjoy any type of macaroni. There are over thirty-five hundred different shapes of pasta to choose from, and they all taste good to me. One of the things I learned on this holiday is what those cute Italian names really mean.

> *Spaghetti* means little twines.
> *Linguine* means little tongues.
> *Fettucine* means little ribbons.
> *Vermicelli* means little worms.
> *Capellini* means little hairs.

I like the Italian name better than the meaning. Plus, there are a lot of fun things to do with macaroni other than eating it.

Many arts and crafts projects begin with a great piece of pasta. Have your daughter make a necklace out of rigatoni or elbows. Get an inexpensive wooden picture frame and glue different pastas on it. Have your kids glue small pieces together and make a picture. The different pastas even come in colors to make it more enjoyable.

Finally, no Macaroni Day would be complete without making the kids' favorite meal; most would think of macaroni and cheese. But I branded my concoction "Daddy's Mix and Magic" and wouldn't let my kids see my secret recipe. Happily, they totally loved it. Because you bought this book, I will trust you with the recipe. It is simply egg noodles and *extra* butter and *extra* salt. As a marketing professional, I branded it with my name to make it a little extra special.

Slurpee Day

July 11

This is not so much an homage to the famous convenience store chain whose name initially represented its hours of operation. The chain started with one store, in Dallas, Texas, in 1927. In 1946, it began to use 7-11 as its name to let customers know that the store would be open from 7:00 a.m. to 11:00 p.m., which was unheard of for store operating hours at that time. At one point, the chain boasted over thirty-nine thousand stores. But this is not about the chain; this is about the Slurpee. I love this drink. So every 7/11, we head down to a local 7-11 and pick one up for each of us. Again, some things are that simple.

Lollipop Day

July 20

According to gone-ta-popp.com,

> The idea of a hard candy on a stick is fairly simple. And, it is probable that the lollipop has been invented and reinvented numerous times. The word "lolly-pop" dates to 1784, but initially referred to soft, rather than hard candy. The term probably derived from the term "lolly" (tongue) and "pop" (slap). The first references to the lollipop in its modern context date to the 1920s. The first confectioneries that closely resemble what we call lollipops date to the Middle Ages, when the nobility would often eat boiled sugar with the aid of sticks or handles. The invention of the modern lollipop is still something of a mystery, but a number of American companies in the early twentieth century have laid claim to it.

This is surely the day to try a bunch of lollipops, including that really big one!

Parents' Day

July 31 (or, the fourth Sunday in July)

According to parentsday.com, many Americans are unaware that our nation has a new day of commemoration called Parents' Day. This is good news for America's parents and families. In 1994 President Bill Clinton signed into law the resolution unanimously adopted by the US Congress establishing the fourth Sunday of every July as Parents' Day, a perennial day of commemoration similar to Mother's Day and Father's Day.

According to the Congressional Resolution, Parents' Day is established for "recognizing, uplifting, and supporting the role of parents in the rearing of children."

To me, this is our chance to get the kids to do everything we want them to do for us, unlike like the other 364 days a year, when we are taking care of them. I treat it just like another birthday, but both parents get to ask for things the same day and join in running the kids ragged. As Jackie Gleason would have said, "How sweet it is."

It's up to you how you want to enjoy this day, but I believe there is a lot of fetching, hugging, kissing, foot massaging, cleaning, washing, face scrubbing, and more, that can be done without much effort.

August

Favorite Day

August 3

This is a very simple day to put together a listing of your children's favorite things. I chose August 3 because there are eight letters in "favorite" and three letters in "day." Very scientific. So, you can give them a chance to list their favorite things in each of the following categories:

Food	Game	Thing to Do	Subject	Store	Fruit
Song	Teacher	Holiday	Joke	Animal	Vegetable
Friend	TV Show	Memory	Restaurant	Hobby	Dessert

You can add or delete as you see fit, but this is your children's way to identify how they are changing over the years. My son asked me the other day, "Dad, do you remember when my favorite food was pizza from Chuck E. Cheese's? I never think about that place anymore." Now, he loves a Japanese steak house. This is too bad for me, because the pizza was much less expensive.

Awesome August Adventure Day

The first or second weekend in August

During May Day Play Day, I said the important thing was that the kids had the choice of what we did. For Awesome August, the parents are back in control! But obviously, knowing your own kids, you get to steer everything the right way for maximum fun.

The adventure starts with advanced planning on your part regarding what you want to do. In my family, we typically started with donuts (no more than two each) to up the sugar levels. And I was not above eating a few more to match my energy level to theirs.

Once we got home from the donut shop, I had a treasure hunt planned and ready to go. This time, since it's August and, I hope, nice and warm, you have them go outside for the treasure hunt. Take small pieces of paper and write one letter of each of your kids' names on each. Apply some scotch tape, and tape the letters on various places. Tree trunks, gutters, patio furniture, rocks, side of the house, and doors all make excellent places to look. When they come back with each of the letters, you should have one small present ready for them.

The adventure continues with something you can do as a family that is different or that is only available in your area for a short while. August was always a time when the state fair was in town, so that was a natural fun adventure. My kids mostly liked the rides, and they all liked the midway games. I tried to pick games for them to play that I knew they could win. For example, when shooting the water pistols at the clown and making a balloon pop or the horse race, try to play with your child when it's just the two of you. You can miss on purpose, and he or she can win; it costs far less than having your kid play against ten other kids at the same time when the odds are tough.

If there isn't a fair nearby, the planetarium, the aquarium, and/or laser tag, are all usually within driving distance. Or, depending on your own level of interest, fishing, camping, hiking, or swimming can be ways to create excitement in the summer.

Remember, parents, these holidays are a little indulgent in every respect, so let your kids have fun with the food selections, too. If you bring along some snacks on your own, allow them to experience some crazy foods, such as corn dogs, elephant ears, kettle corn, or whatever is available and new. If it's new to your kids, it will keep their minds open to new adventures.

You can also change it up by patronizing a local attraction that you may have taken for granted or never seen. While living in Detroit, we went to Frankenmuth, where my son loved to ride the steamboat, went to the zoo, visited the IMAX theater, or walked through the Detroit Art Museum. In Richmond, we visited the air museum, attended the horse races, and took in a few Richmond Braves baseball games. In Memphis, a little trip down the Mississippi River was just the thing.

Afterward, we liked watching the ducks in the Drake Hotel, eating ribs downtown on Beale Street, and going to a Memphis Tigers football game. In Philadelphia, we never tired of seeing the Liberty Bell and Independence Hall, or taking a short train ride to New York City to see the Statue of Liberty. Once, we just rode our bikes for five miles to get to a McDonald's for a Happy Meal.

The adventure is in the planning and the doing of something a little different. You will enjoy getting out with your kids and seeing the fun things your town has to offer.

This event usually takes up a few hours of the day, and everyone is probably going to be a little tired, so you'll want to wrap it up with some winding-down event. I liked Putt-Putt golf, or an arcade palace. You might like a small museum tour, or coming back to watch your favorite movie at the house. I liked to finish things off with a fun family dinner of pizza, or maybe grilling some hamburgers and hot dogs. Afterward, we'd pile the kids in the car, one last time, for ice cream at their favorite place. Then the day is over!

The fun part is that it is a family adventure that really isn't hard to put together. The costs are up to you. You can really be a hero with your kids, as they get older, if you invite one of their friends to join in the fun. Most families do not do anything like you will be doing, and once your kids talk about all the other fun you've found in this book, they will think, "You are the greatest parent in the world."

Another self-indulgent aspect of this day is to make the kids say, out loud, how much fun they had by shouting out:

ME:	THEM:
Who had fun today?	Me!
Who is the greatest dad in the world?	You!
Who wants to do this again?	Me!

It did get interesting, when my kids started bringing friends along, to listen to the other kids, who were not related to me, proclaim that I was the greatest dad in the world.

Marshmallow Day

August 30

This day is a time for camping out, usually in the backyard or basement I used to set up a tent and, of course, before turning off the flashlights and jumping into the sleeping bags, we always roasted marshmallows outside or in the fireplace. I personally like mine burnt and aflame, but my kids liked to gradually roast them until the marshmallow was brown. The key to an enjoyable roasting was finding a long stick that was equipped with enough offshoots to accommodate several marshmallows together.

The other benefit of the day was that it gave everyone time to just talk about things, with no distractions of TV, phones, or music, while sitting outside looking at stars or drifting off to sleep. This would be the perfect time to teach the kids a little about the constellations, and the Big and Little Dippers, and Orion's belt, too. Since both of my children are in the zodiac sign of Cancer, I showed them how to find that particular constellation. All thanks to marshmallows.

September

Labor Day

Traditionally the first Monday in September, Labor Day is celebrated by most Americans as the symbolic end of summer. The holiday is often regarded as a day of rest and parties.

For this Labor Day, the tables are turned a little, and the kids get to be the laborers. That's right! A day where they wait on you! It's supposed to be a day of rest for those of us who work all year, and kids tend to play all year. So, put away your guilt and use the kids to run errands around the house. Maybe they can get you a cold drink, set the table, fold a few clothes, tidy up the house, get the ice cubes, and many more things. Depending on the ages of the kids, ask them to do anything you feel they can handle. Avoid asking them to cook the burgers on the grill if your children are too young; you don't want yours burned!

Opposite Day (Part 2)

September 6

The sister to this is June 9, when the numbers 6 and 9 are both inverted. If you go back to June, you can reread all the things available for Opposite Day. It's the only holiday that appears twice. Just being "opposite" of normal, I guess.

Opposite Day was good once in a while, and, like I said before, my kids enjoyed being the "parents," but they didn't really go all out for this one. That's not to say it was bad; your kids may take this to a whole new level and grasp some concepts mine didn't. Or, your creativeness may be significantly better than mine. It was a fun day to try things new and get the kids to think about changing the routine and opening their minds to new concepts.

Remember one thing, Labor Day and Opposite Day can be very close together, so enjoy your own creativity and go opposite on another day. It doesn't even have to be in September!

Teddy Bear Day

September 9

According to holidayinsights.com,

> The origin of the teddy bear was during the early 1900s. Theodore Roosevelt was in office as President of the United States. He was a hunter. While hunting in Mississippi in 1902, he refused to shoot a small bear. *The Washington Post* picked up on this story, and made a cartoon of the event. Toy storeowners Morris and Rose Michtom wrote to President Roosevelt for permission to call their stuffed animals "Teddy Bears." Teddy bears became wildly popular. Their company went on to become the Ideal Toy Company, one of the largest toy companies in the world.

So to celebrate this day, we know all kids have at least one favorite teddy bear, a best friend, that they take to bed with them. My daughter's was called Night Night bear; she still has her, and she really needs a good cleaning. My son's was simply named Teddy. But on Teddy Bear Day, your child may do everything with his or her favorite bear—watch TV together, read together, and have dinner and talk together. Most importantly, we'll see a nice picture of the family together, with our favorite animal of all . . . the Teddy Bear.

September Search

By this time, school is officially back in session throughout the country, and the kids are in that in-between time of summer vacation hangover, meeting new friends, getting up early for the bus, and, *ugh*, homework. Toward the end of September, I like to engage their brains and their bodies in a good, old-fashioned treasure hunt. This treasure hunt is a little different than the others; I try to get them to really think about the clues they're given. I use yellow Post-It notes and leave clues around the house for them to find. For the younger kids, it can be as simple as this list of clues.

> (On a sign placed right at the entrance to the house): "Look under the lamp in your bedroom."
> (Under the lamp you can leave a note that might say): "Go to the kitchen and look behind the toaster."

You get the idea. The number of clues might reflect the number of your child's age (another recurrence of this). The last clue could look something like this:

> "The last clue is to give your mom and dad five hugs and kisses!" (Or, instead of five, you could write however many years old your child is.)

The treat for finishing the search might be your child's favorite candy bar, movie tickets, or a song to download.

As your kids get older, make the clues a little harder. For example:

> "Go to the table of faces." (This was a reference to a small table we had with plenty of pictures of our family.)
> "Look under the biggest noisemaker in the house." (My piano.)
> "Go to the worldwide answer machine." (The computer.)
> "Open the door to the coldest place in the house." (The refrigerator.)

The last clue will remain the same as before. So, get all the hugs and kisses you can!

October

Oktoberfest

This is not about the real Oktoberfest, which is one of the most famous events in Germany. It is an opportunity to sample German foods, such as "Würstl (sausages) along with Brezn (pretzels), Knödel (potato or bread dumplings), Kasspatzn (cheese noodles), Reiberdatschi (potato pancakes), Sauerkraut or Blaukraut (red cabbage), or Hendl (chicken)," which are all listed in Wikipedia's entry for Oktoberfest.

And, of course, let's not forget the root beer, for the kids.

It's really about allowing your kids to experience a different culture and sample the local foods. My version of Oktoberfest is simply a festival held in October. Visit Chinatown, Little Italy, Irish pubs, or the local eateries of fame, which can all be included in this event. If you are in the South, go to a famous barbeque place. If you are in Chicago, go find a traditional deep-dish pizza. Cheesesteaks will serve in Philadelphia, and ribs are just the thing if you are in Memphis.

Certainly, if there is a local German Oktoberfest party going on, take your family to enjoy it. Offer them a map to study to see where Germany is located, and you'll expose them to some world geography, also.

Dictionary Day

October 16

As my children began getting older, I liked to play an easy, interesting game with them by browsing the dictionary, selecting a word, and seeing if anyone could come up with the meaning of it. I'm sure there are a few board games developed with this simple premise, but all we needed was my old, worn-out dictionary. Whoever guessed correctly received a piece of candy. (With Halloween right around the corner, we had stocked up on our favorite candy already.) The origin of this holiday, which is really supposed to honor Noah Webster, the father of the American dictionary, was in response to Oktoberfest. My kids told me repeatedly there wasn't a "k" in October, and I was spelling it incorrectly. Since spelling seemed to be of interest, I developed Dictionary Day. It transformed into spelling *and* understanding the meaning of words. It also gave me a chance to use my 1975 dictionary, which was awarded to me by Brockport Central School for outstanding scholastic achievement, and brag a bit to my kids. To this day, the word "wame" is one of the words coming from the game that I still remember the meaning of . . . belly!

Magic Day

October 31

National Magic Day is celebrated on October 31, in honor of Harry Houdini, who died on Halloween in 1926. I observed this day a few days before Halloween.

So, what did I do for this day? Well, when I was a teenager, my brother-in-law was very good at card tricks. He knew several tricks, and, one afternoon, he taught them to me. I practiced those and became pretty good at using them whenever a deck of cards was available. Now, I am not a magician by any means, but these tricks always astounded my kids. So, every Magic Day, I would teach them one of the card tricks. In addition, I was a sucker for real magic tricks. I desperately wanted to know how they were performed; I even went so far as to buy some from the magic store, just to see how they were done.

Do you know any tricks? They will be very enjoyable on this day. I was sworn to keep my brother-in-law's card tricks in the family, so *you* will have to make a little magic on your own.

Halloween

October 31

Halloween is observed on October 31 and includes activities such as trick-or-treating, going to costume parties, carving pumpkins, visiting haunted houses, telling scary stories, and watching horror films.

I like to call this Eat As Much Candy As You Want Day. Before you cringe at that statement, please relax, bear with me, and allow me to explain. I believe Halloween is about many things, not just candy. And at the end of this section, you'll see why I call this Eat As Much Candy As You Want Day. I have friends who truly go all out—with coffins on the front lawn and gravestones in the shrubs—and they dress up in costume in the doorways and scare trick-or-treaters, as they hand out candy. I applaud anyone who takes Halloween to that level, because Halloween has become something of an adult holiday for partying. And, as you already know, that is not what this book is about.

I will admit, however, that this holiday is almost like a dress rehearsal for Christmas.

I like to decorate the exterior of my house in orange, orange, and more orange. Hanging orange lights on the shrubs lets everyone know that you are serious about Halloween. Because decorating with lights on Halloween isn't very common, this is a way for your kids to be recognized as cool by other kids in the neighborhood. When I first started this decorating, we were living in a home in Virginia, and our house was at the end of the cul-de-sac. If you turned onto our street, our house was the first to be seen. Since no one else really decorated with lights, our house stood out. Many homes are lit up with Christmas lights, but only my kids' house had lights for Halloween—always a conversation starter in class or with the teacher. Of course, be prepared for plenty of trick-or-treaters to come to the door.

In addition to the tree and shrub lights, I always liked to place large pumpkin lights around the door, ghost stickers in the windows, large illuminated pumpkins and ghosts by the entryway to the front door, and a couple of scarecrows and pumpkins in the yard. Top it off with a CD player hidden in the shrubs with some scary noises, and you have the makings of a fun house. I have tried, but ultimately decided against, the fog-making machines because they just don't seem to work when you want them to. People smarter than I am might be able to make a sensor device for the fog machines, which could activate the fog when kids are coming up the driveway.

To me, the pumpkins are the main attraction for the kids, though. Because this book is about making an event out of ordinary things, the selection of the pumpkins is key in this process. Anyone can go to the grocery store, pick up some pumpkins from a box, and call it a day. If you are fortunate enough to live near a "pumpkin patch," that's the place to be; the prices are a little higher than at the grocery store, but there are hay rides, corn mazes to walk through, a haunted village of some sort, and hundreds of pumpkins, some weighing in at over five hundred pounds. These will *not* be found at your local grocer.

When leaving the pumpkin patch, you should go home with a pumpkin for every member of the family—Papa Pumpkin, Mama Pumpkin, Brother Pumpkin, and Sister Pumpkin. How you let the kids choose their own pumpkins is up to you and your budget. Since many pumpkin patches weigh the pumpkins, clean off any dirt before the weighing process, to avoid paying for that. I ended up letting the kids pick any pumpkin they could carry. That put them more in line with a smaller one and kept my prices low. I enjoyed selecting the Papa Pumpkin. I routinely chose the biggest, roundest, orangest pumpkin I could carry. Make sure that the pumpkins you pick have strong, sturdy stems. If the stem breaks off easily, the pumpkin is old, and you should pass on it. Look for pumpkins with greenish stems, because that's an indicator that they haven't been sitting around too long. In the pumpkin patch, take your time and walk toward the back. Most people are reluctant to walk too far, but you won't find the best pumpkins where the hayride drops you off. Walk farther away because that's part of the fun, too, of finding that perfect pumpkin. You will be surprised at what your kids decide to bring home; I always was.

Carving the pumpkins is a family affair when the kids get older. But using a knife to carve your pumpkin isn't the wisest thing to do around a little kid. The knife may slip, or fall, and create a safety hazard for small children. But little ones can participate. Have the kids pick out an easy face to carve, draw it on the pumpkin, ask them if they like it, and then carve it. You can find some easy designs online. Again, you will see how some kids like happy faces with triangle eyes and a few teeth, while others would prefer an evil, scary face. The intricate drawings and carving tools that come with pumpkin carving sets are fun, but they can prolong the process. Personally, I like big eyes and a gaping mouth, so the candle inside is easy to see.

The story of the jack o' lantern has its origins in Irish folklore. As I read on Squidoo.com,

Jack was a crafty farmer who tricked the Devil into climbing a tall tree. When the Devil reached the highest branch, Jack carved a large cross in the trunk, making it impossible for the Devil to climb down.

In exchange for help getting out of the tree, the Devil promised never to tempt Jack with evil again. When Jack died, he was turned away from Heaven for his sins and turned away from Hell because of his trickery. Condemned to wander the earth without rest, Jack carved out one of his turnips, took an ember from the devil, and used it for a lantern to light his way. He became known as "Jack of the Lantern."

Of course, the next phase, which *everyone* loves, is cleaning the inside of the pumpkin and separating the seeds from the pulp. All I can say about this is that it's slimy, slimy, and slimy. I use a spoon to scrape everything out and a colander to put it all in. Next, rinse everything off to separate the seeds.

To make a good batch of pumpkin seeds, we use this recipe:

1. Rinse pumpkin seeds under cold water and pick out the pulp and strings. (This is easiest just after you've removed the seeds from the pumpkin, before the pulp has dried.)
2. Place the pumpkin seeds in a single layer on an oiled baking sheet or omit the oil and coat with nonstick cooking spray.
3. Sprinkle with salt and bake at 325 degrees Fahrenheit until toasted, for about twenty-five minutes, checking and stirring after ten minutes.
4. Let cool and store in an air-tight container.

A note on costumes: the earlier you shop for them, the better off you'll be. Shop as soon as possible for your kids' costumes, before the stores begin to run out of popular items. It can be frustrating for your child, who wants to be Spiderman but can't because that costume is all sold out. Remember a few things, too. It can be cold when the kids go trick-or-treating, so, to make sure your children can wear warm clothes under their costumes, purchase costumes that are one size too big.

When you go trick-or-treating, remember that younger kids tire out easily. So, pace yourself, and it can't hurt to bring along a wagon. At the beginning of the night, I used it to carry refreshments for me and my friends, but it really came in handy later for the kids to ride in when they were too tired to walk. When the kids get older, they can dump their extra candy in the wagon while walking, so it's easier for them to run from house to house.

After all the candy has been collected, and we return home, I like to see who shares and who doesn't. We generally separate all the candy out by types. For example, we put all the Reese's Peanut Butter Cups together, all the Snickers bars together, all the Kit Kats together, and so on. Check all the candy to make sure it hasn't been tampered with; throw out any apples or other fruit that someone might have tampered with. I like Sweet Tarts and York Peppermint Patties, but I always let the kids take what they want first, and then see what they give me.

Handing out candy to trick-or-treaters is tricky. I don't believe teenagers should be out getting candy. In fact, I think that all kids' events are for children under the age of twelve. Now, I also believe that, the younger the child is, the more fun Halloween is for them So, for the little trick-or-treaters, I throw out the rule of one piece of candy per child, and instead I implement the rule of "take as much as you can with one hand!"

That said, I would love to be the Candy Man. The Candy Man lived in our community, outside Memphis, Tennessee, and worked for a candy company. Every Halloween, he brought home boxes and boxes of candy, to pass out to kids. He set up tables for the different types of candy he had, and he didn't just have bite-sized pieces; no, he had the monster-sized suckers that take six years to lick. He also had long strings of candy and samples of candies that weren't on the market yet. Everyone in the neighborhood knew where the Candy Man lived—what a great tradition for him.

Now, finally, let's get to the part detailing what is Eat As Much Candy As You Want Day. When I started my parenting journey, on Halloween I didn't want them eating a ton of candy all night and would try to stop them after I thought they'd had enough. This was always met with whining, trying to eat more, or sneaking it away. So, with a little reverse psychology, one Halloween I said they could eat as much as they wanted, warning that if they ate too much they would get really sick. But it was up to them.

Now, maybe this only happens with my kids, but before, when they were stopped after eating ten pieces of candy, they would whine and whine for more. When they were told that they could have as much as they wanted, they ate about thirteen pieces and were done. Whether I took away all the fun or not, they were done when they were done, and they put the candy away. I got what I wanted, and then, to please Mom, I ended up taking a lot of it to work, where my coworkers and I nibbled on it for several days, sometimes weeks.

November

Veterans Day

November 11

Veteran's Day is an annual holiday honoring military veterans. My father served in World War II and shared the horrors of war that many simply do not know about. Many years later, I still have the US flag that was presented to me upon his death. For kids, this holiday is for learning that, while untold numbers of people have helped make this a great country, it is our veterans who, on this day, deserve to be recognized for risking their lives so that we may enjoy so many things.

We have bought many small flags and placed them around our sidewalks, like on Memorial Day, to show a simple tribute to these wonderful men and women. The kids put them in the ground and pick them up the next day.

Pizza Day

November 12

This is the day we make our favorite pizza at home, or we get one from the surprisingly popular "Take and Bake" pizza parlors popping up all over. Similar to Hamburger Day, Pizza days are plentiful over the year. November 12 is National Pizza Day with the works (except anchovies) while September 5 is National Cheese Pizza Day, but I am sticking with my date, because my favorite toppings are pepperoni, sausage, green peppers, mushrooms, and sometimes black olives. It's not the works, but it's close enough for me. And my understanding is that the Wednesday prior to Thanksgiving is the day when more pizzas are bought than any other day of the year because who wants to make another meal when the big event is the next day? So, now you get to beat the rush and enjoy your own pizza at home. I recommend you find your own special recipe for a homemade pizza, but if you need one, the following recipe for a simple dough is from smittenkitchen.com:

> 1½ cups flour (can replace up to half of this with whole wheat flour)
> 1 teaspoon salt
> 3/4 teaspoon active dry yeast
> 1/2 cup lukewarm water (may need up to 1 or 2 tablespoons more)
> 1 tablespoon olive oil
> This is for a thin crust, but double the above if you like a thicker, breadier crust.

Stir dry ingredients, including yeast, in a large bowl. Add water and olive oil, stirring mixture into as close to a ball as you can. Dump all clumps and floury bits onto a lightly floured surface and knead everything into a homogeneous ball.

Knead it for just a minute or two. Lightly oil the bowl (a spritz of cooking spray perfectly does the trick) where you had mixed it—one-bowl recipe!—dump the dough in, turn it over so all sides are coated, cover it in plastic wrap and leave it undisturbed for an hour or two, until it has doubled in size.

Gently press the air out of the dough with the palm of your hands. Fold the piece into an approximate ball shape, and let it sit under that plastic wrap for twenty more minutes.

Sprinkle a baking sheet with cornmeal and preheat your oven to its top temperature. Roll out the pizza, toss on whatever topping and seasonings you like. (Always err on the side of skimpy with toppings so as to not weigh down the dough too much, or, if you have multiple toppings, keep them very thinly sliced.)

Bake it for about ten minutes, until it's lightly blistered and impossible to resist.

Or, if you are feeling particularly adventurous, try Cici's Pizza, which is an all you can eat parlor, and have everyone try at least one slice of pizza from each pie they put out. You can substitute your favorite pizza parlor, but trying something different is the variation for Pizza Day.

Thanksgiving

Thanksgiving, celebrated on the fourth Thursday in November, has officially been an annual tradition since 1863, when, according to Wikipedia, "President Lincoln proclaimed a national day of thanksgiving to be celebrated on Thursday, November 26th." Thanksgiving is one of the "big six" major holidays of the year.

It is a time for giving thanks, spending time with family, watching football games and parades, and enjoying great amounts of turkey, stuffing, mashed potatoes, and cranberry sauce.

Wikipedia informs us that "the modern Thanksgiving holiday traces its origins from a 1621 celebration at the Plymouth Plantation, in Massachusetts, where the early settlers held a harvest feast after a successful growing season." If you recall from the July chapter, though, the first Thanksgiving was celebrated in Virginia in 1619. I am just checking with you to ensure you have read every word!

As a holiday for kids, the only thing that rivals the family celebration is volunteering to help others and learning to be grateful for our many blessings. There was nothing as uplifting to me as volunteering in a food shelter to peel potatoes, which I like to do, and know that my efforts are helping to feed hundreds of people that day. When your kids are old enough, I encourage you to volunteer at a food kitchen together and encourage them to give back to their community.

I am thankful, as a Dallas Cowboys fan, that watching Dallas play every Thanksgiving Day permits me to wear my Cowboys jersey—all my family members have one too—and root for the Boys to win. I spent seven years in Detroit, also (and, yes, I can root for the Lions, too). There I had the wonderful opportunity to participate in the Thanksgiving Day parade, as a balloon handler, and that was a tiring thrill. Spinning those massive balloons (Elmo was mine), in a ten-person team, was very enjoyable and memorable. I hope that your team plays on Thanksgiving (if not, root for the Cowboys and the Lions) and that you enjoy the football and feast celebrations.

Many like to give thanks, around the dinner table, for things they really appreciate. Since your children look to you as a role model, identifying at least one thing you are thankful for (your spouse, kids, music, sports, books, family, pets, career, home, etc.) really sets the tone for the holiday and helps focus the kids' thoughts and puts a little more meaning into the celebration.

Hookey Day

November 30

Also known as Stay At Home When You Are Well Day, this is one of those days when I do my Christmas shopping and get everything ready for the big month. Being able to plan out your career vacation time in advance really helps with this and if your kids can afford to miss a day of school, you have the makings of another great family adventure.

This family shopping day is enjoyable because your family will know you will be doing something together, and they are getting a day out of school. The one rule for shopping that I try to enforce is that we need to be there when the first store opens. That way, it will seem as if you are on a schedule, and you'll have time to visit all the stores on your list. This is like Black Friday, but without the long lines and the masses of people.

December

Christmas

Christmas is "the big one," the holiday that inspired the writing of this book. The other eleven months of the year feature multiple holidays to surprise and delight the little ones, but this event is so big that it occupies the whole month! As a result, this chapter is organized differently than the others.

Christmas Day is a holiday observed on December 25, and according to Wikipedia.com:

> Popular modern customs of the holiday include gift giving, Christmas music and caroling, an exchange of Christmas cards, church celebrations, a special meal, and the display of various decorations, including Christmas trees, lights, nativity scenes, garlands, wreaths, mistletoe, and holly. In addition, several closely related and often interchangeable figures, known as Santa Claus, Father Christmas, Saint Nicholas and Kris Kringle among other names, are associated with bringing gifts to children during the Christmas season

My holiday traditions for Christmas are born out of the point of view that the season is a magical time for children. Feel free to agree, disagree, add, modify, adjust, or completely ignore the customs that don't fit into your lifestyle or beliefs. This chapter is not about the Christmas season's religious components; rather, it is about the wonderful outpouring of joy and goodwill that the season inspires. It is about offering you activities you can do with your kids, based on what I did with mine that made this season memorable for me.

Christmas Trees

The experience of searching for, and ultimately finding, the perfect tree for your home and family is the first part of the enjoyment of the holiday. Letting your kids experience the selection, location, and decoration of the tree will create cherished memories for them.

There are many different types of trees to choose from; the most common Christmas trees are firs, pines, and spruces. Each tree has distinct traits, and they all vary in fragrance, needle retention, and softness, and, of course, price. Douglas fir, Scotch pine, and blue spruce are my favorites in these categories. Many families enjoy making a big event of selecting their tree, and they plan a trip to a tree farm to choose and cut down their own tree. The main advantage to this method is that the tree will be as fresh as can be, and it will last well into the month. I prefer the less rigorous option of going to a local tee lot and picking out the best one.

However, if you are going to a tree farm, here are a few tips to remember:

1. Call before you go to make sure that they are open, and they have trees available. (Weather could be a factor in tree availability.)
2. Ask if they provide sawing equipment or if they will cut the tree for you, if you want.
3. Will they bag it and transport it to your car, or do you have to do that also?
4. Many tree farms have hay rides, Santa visits, restaurants, and gift shops to make your trip more enjoyable. Calling the farm to ascertain this and asking how long it will take to do everything will help you plan your time (and the kids' attention spans) better.
5. Before you bag up the tree, shake it vigorously. It will have been outside for a long time, and critters, such as spiders and other bugs, like to make the branches their home. You probably don't want to introduce a fresh batch of uninvited guests into your car or house.

There are many more tips that can be gleaned online, such as having gloves, things to kneel on, and appropriate tools, and I encourage you to do a little homework before driving to the farm.

If you purchase a tree from a local parking lot, church, or school, you will want to check for similar things to what I mention above. You will also need to ask yourself, *How tall should the tree be?* My rule of thumb is to start with the height of the room and subtract two feet. That allows room for the ornament on top of the tree as well as extra height you will get from the stand you place it in. You can ask the attendant you buy it from to trim a little more off the trunk, if necessary. You want the bottom trimmed a few inches anyway to open it up so it will absorb water when you bring it home and so it fits inside the stand. Also when selecting a tree, place your fingers inside the tree, maybe four to six inches back from the tips of the branches, and run your hand up and down the branches to confirm that the needles are not falling off. Vendors will *always* tell you that the trees are freshly cut, but, in a few days, the vendors will be gone, and you want the freshest tree, not the one that is turning brown before Christmas Day.

For those of you who enjoy the new crop of artificial trees and their relative ease of assembly, predecoration, and needles that never fall off, I say *bah, humbug*! Those trees are very convenient and have great appeal, but the selection process is gone, the family time together is now just bringing it up from the basement, and the uniqueness of the tree (size, color, and smell) is missing. If you have little kids at home, nothing beats the smell of a new tree in your house and the fun of decorating it as *the showpiece* of your holiday.

Ornaments

Angels are very pretty, but I urge that you look at tree drawings by youngsters and ask yourself, *What's on top?* A star!

Each child in the family should also have his or her own unique ornament, featuring his or her name. Let your child choose the color, the size, and the shape, and let him or her choose where to hang it on the tree. It should be the child's moment of pride in the tree and in how it's decorated. Those can be the *first* ornaments placed on the tree.

Today, there are many different types of ornaments to enjoy or to demonstrate your pride. Whether it is your favorite sports team, some snowmen, a few animal figures, some religious objects, or the places you visited, I highly encourage you to use ornaments that mean something to *you*. Why did you decide to hang that ornament on the tree? Is it pretty, or is it a gift your son received on his first Christmas? Perhaps you have a collection of ornaments from your own childhood? Give them importance by telling a story each year.

Another way to involve your kids is to let them pick out *one* ornament each year that they might like to have for their trees when they're older. Watch the progression of their selections as they get older, and then, when they leave the nest (*hopefully*), let them have the ornaments they chose so that they may continue the tradition as they get older.

One of my unique, favorite ornaments is the pickle. This is a German tradition which states that the last ornament placed on the tree is the pickle, and when Santa comes, he moves it, and the child who finds it first in the morning gets a special treat, such as be the first to open a present (or receive an extra little present, etc.). It is a nice tradition designed to encourage the kids to appreciate the ornaments and the beauty of the tree, rather than the presents.

Tree Lights

To me, your lights on the tree should have no blinkers! I believe a tree should be soothing and peaceful to look at when all the other lights are turned off. Blinking lights always reminded me of a flashing warning light at an intersection. My father loved the blinking lights, and so we always decorated our trees with them, but remember, this is about *your* traditions and what you like to do with your family, so embrace what makes you happy. I love trees decorated exclusively in white lights, but I found colors were more appealing to kids. And since this book is about kids, that means I'm putting my money on *colors*!

Stockings

Yes. One for each family member (including pets) with either the family members' names on them or stockings that they chose themselves and will use every year.

Outdoor Lights

Outdoor lights are wonderful, but, again, I am not a fan of blinkers! My preference is to decorate the house to make it stand out. Now, it wasn't always this way with me. I didn't put up my first exterior light until my daughter was about three years old. She was looking out our front window at a neighbor's house and said, "Daddy, why can't our house look that pretty?" That started it, and then my passion (or fever) for the task intensified, as more and more lights started going up. I like trees decorated with green along the trunks and white lights on the branches. We have red candy canes (Candy Cane Lane) along the walkway and reindeer on the grass, to give some depth, and pretty white lights on all the shrubs. How much is too much? I'm not sure there can be too much. Is my house seen from space? Maybe.

I admit I may go a little overboard on my exterior lights. It takes me about eight hours to put them up, and it always takes me lots of time to figure out how to connect the electrical cords so they don't blow any fuses. It takes about five hours to take them down. Helpful hint: time shouldn't be a problem for you when putting up the lights if you pick a warm day. I am incredibly impatient, and yet, I tell myself, *I won't be bothered if the lights are tangled, and I am enjoying the day.* (I have learned to put them all away by wrapping the lights around the holders they came in, so that they are not tangled when I pull them out the following year.) Also, remember to test the lights *before* you put them up!

These lights are for the kids, but for a month or so, I guarantee that you will really enjoy driving up to your home, after a long day at work, and seeing the fruits of your labor. When taking my lights down, I have had several neighbors, whom I did not know, stop by and tell me how much they enjoyed them. They had told their friends about my house and how beautiful it looked. This was my way of being the Candy Man (see chapter titled "October").

Presents

Santa did not wrap his presents to my children. That's how they knew who they are from. This is probably the most frustrating area, as somehow Santa has different ideas for different kids. Oh, well.

I also wanted Santa to deliver no more than three presents to each child. Parents are the heroes. Delight in that!

Twelve Days of Christmas

Most people believe that the twelve days of Christmas refers to the days before Christmas, but they are really the twelve days *after* Christmas, from December 25 to January 5, marking the beginning of Epiphany. For others, their main reference to the twelve days of Christmas is the carol that we hear every year, for which I can never remember any lyrics beyond the five golden rings.

I observe the time frame a little differently. This began gradually, as I noticed that, for smaller kids, opening all the presents on Christmas Eve or Day started to get boring for them. They couldn't maintain their excitement level, and they wore down too quickly, so I made up the twelve days of Christmas, where each child could open one present each day for the twelve days leading up to Christmas morning. Now, we were fortunate in that there were several uncles, aunts, grandparents, and friends who could provide enough presents to choose from. We noticed that the kids got excited every day. They enjoyed that one present—no clothes, please, for little ones—and we got to enjoy the looks on their faces for thirteen straight days.

Reindeer Dust

Yes, you have to make sure that the reindeer can spot your house, so Santa doesn't miss you! A wonderful little mix of oatmeal and sprinkles, when dropped outside, gives the sleigh-pulling reindeer a little extra help to see, and smell, their way to your house. Reindeer can smell food up to one hundred miles away, and this concoction lets them smell *and* see their way to your home. Don't sprinkle too much in any one place; it is best to spread it around your house or apartment building. Have the kids make their own and spread it around, all the while enjoying the outdoors.

Feeding Santa and the Reindeer

Everyone forgets the reindeer, but they do love carrots. They don't care much for the machine-lathed kind that comes in plastic bags from the store. They need the ones that have the green stalks on them and are fully grown. It takes a little longer for them, but it's what they like the best. Make sure there are nine of them, also. Your kids can count them out in the store. Later, they can elect which bunch to provide.

Santa does indeed get milk and cookies. My preference is to make the easy-bake ones together and have the kids help with the Pillsbury cooking dough, but, as everybody knows, Santa eats anything.

Tracking Santa

The North American Aerospace Defense Command website, www. noradsanta.org, shows where Santa is all over the world. It's fun to see where he is and keep tabs on that fast, jolly guy. It is also another way to expose kids to the map of the world. Caution, the website shows Santa moving so fast that it will inspire the following question, "How does Santa travel that fast?" Of course, I was completely honest and told them I had no idea. He must be able to stop time, somehow, precisely at midnight.

Bedtime Story

The only one we read on Christmas Eve is *'Twas the Night Before Christmas*. We have a nice hardcover edition that we bring out once a year.

Kids need to be asleep or Santa doesn't come, and ten o'clock seemed like a good time for bed.

Letter from Santa

I always looked forward to getting that typed letter from Santa thanking us for the carrots. (Common subjects included: one reindeer that was always particularly hungry, how delicious the cookies were, and the lessons Santa wanted our kids to do. He also encouraged the kids to study more, to be nice to their sibling, to do certain chores, and to remember that their parents loved them the most. Here is a sample letter we received from Santa:

Dear Taylor and Zachary,

Thank you for the cookies, milk, and carrots, for my reindeer. Blitzen could not get enough to eat tonight and, actually, ate three carrots. Fortunately, the others were full from previous stops and shared the extras. I enjoyed the cookies too; I need to go on a diet tomorrow, after eating all of your delicious treats.

Well, another year has come and gone since my last note to you. My, there have been so many changes in a year. I see you even added a puppy to your family. Zsa Zsa [our puppy's name] and I visited a little tonight while you were both sleeping.

As I have watched you this year, you both are really growing up. You are playing together better, although, you could both share a bit more.

Taylor, I would like you to concentrate more in school this year and keep your grades up. You will be going to a new school, again, when your parents move, and I know you will make a lot of new friends and have so much fun with them.

Zachary, I would like you to also work harder in school. You are very smart, but you need to pay attention to the teacher and listen to instructions really well, so you keep getting high marks.

I only have one last thing, for both of you, please listen to what your parents tell you. They love you more than anyone else in the whole world.

I hope you like your presents this year . . . Remember; I'll be watching you for next year.

Secret Santa:

The Society of Secret Santas is an anonymous group of individuals throughout the world, performing random acts of kindness to those less fortunate. Using their own financial resources, without a tax deduction and without soliciting funds from others, these leaders share their wealth with those in need. They give from their hearts, remaining forever anonymous. To become a Secret Santa, visit their website at http://www.secretsantaworld.net.

The above paragraph comes directly from the Society of Secret Santas website and is dedicated to Larry Stewart, the original Secret Santa. While the website is mostly about financial donations, I believe a Secret Santa is also about warm, considerate people, who give of themselves. Examples of this include stopping to help someone whose car has stalled, helping someone climb stairs with groceries, or just picking up a neighbor's mail when he or she is away on vacation.

In Memphis, there was one particularly harsh storm, and a major limb of one of our trees fell down in the front yard. It was so big that it couldn't be picked up; it needed to be cut. I was not looking forward to all that work, but I was planning to rent a chain saw and work on it the following weekend. One day, I came home from work, and it was gone! A neighbor, who I never even met, sent her college-aged sons down to do it for us. The young men said their mom told them to do it for us because that's what neighbors do. That is a Secret Santa.

Christmas was the catalyst for all the other holidays that culminated in this book. I hope you can add your own family traditions to them, particularly your own spiritual beliefs.

Stay Up as Late as You Want Day (New Year's Eve)

December 31

New Year's Eve is often celebrated with parties and social gatherings, spanning the transition from one year to the next, at midnight. I also call this Stay Up As Late As You Want Day. In our youth, my wife and I really weren't big party animals, and after the kids were born, we preferred staying in with them anyway. I let them stay up til midnight if they could and watch the ball drop in Times Square. (They never made it, until they were ten years old.)

Even though they will probably hate it, give them the words to Auld Lang Syne and sing together.

> Should auld acquaintance be forgot,
> And never brought to mind?
> Should auld acquaintance be forgot,

And days of auld lang syne?
For auld lang syne, my dear
For auld lang syne,
We'll take a cup o' kindness yet
For auld lang syne!

The words *auld lang syne,* translated from an old Scottish dialect, mean "old long ago," and are about love and friendship in times past. "We'll take a cup o' kindness yet" refers to a shared drink, symbolizing friendship. Happy New Year!

At midnight, I also allowed a sip of champagne for each of them (they hated it), and then we would run outside and around our house, counter-clockwise, leaving the front door open to signify letting all the bad luck out of the house and bringing in good luck. They loved that part because they always beat me. If you remember, on January 1, we also ate the twelve cookies for good luck. The kids wanted to eat them immediately, whereas I wanted to wait until the morning and enjoy them with coffee. After a certain age, it seems that recording the ball drop, and watching it the next morning, makes for a more enjoyable evening. Although, every year somehow I manage to make it until midnight.

Other Special Days

Birthdays

The celebration of a child's birthday is the one constant all children love to look forward to. As they grow, it's one question always asked of them, followed by what grade they are in, if they're old enough. Yes, birthdays are about cake, candles, presents, and the "Happy Birthday" song. "Happy Birthday to You" is the most recognized song in the English language, followed by "For He's a Jolly Good Fellow" and "Auld Lang Syne." "Happy Birthday to You" comes from the song "Good Morning to All," which was written and composed by Patty and Mildred Hill in 1893.

This day is also named Whatever You Want To Do Day. That's right, parents; let the child decide what he or she wants to do, and, if within reason and budget, let him or her choose the day. Let your child stay home from school if he or she wants to. *Yes!* You should ask, because most kids really don't want to stay home; they want to enjoy the attention they get from their teachers and friends. So, whatever day you choose to celebrate your child's birthday, let the child be the ruler.

My kids always wanted to start their day with eating donuts. (You can already tell, from this book, that they had a fondness for those fried treats.) Also, early on, until they were about seven or eight years old, they asked for lunch at Chuck E. Cheese's, followed by games. Ultimately we'd head home for the birthday dinner, presents, and cake.

As they grew up, they wanted to try other activities, probably because they were exposed to so many other things during Awesome August Adventure Days. Again, this has to be your child's day. Sometimes, my son wanted to play video games with me for *hours*. My daughter liked going shopping with her friends for *hours*. They know that you are probably doing things you prefer not to, and they will love you all the more for it. Remember, just say, "It's your day," each time. They need to enjoy the power they have.

Once the day is over, they get to sit in the premier chair at the table. It's *the birthday chair*. It should be decorated with helium-filled balloons, streamers on the sides, and a sign on the chair back: Reserved for (your child's name). And it should be at the head of the table. In my house, at the dinner table, we all generally sat at the same place, and I was usually at the head, so the birthday kid got *my* chair, which reinforced the position of prominence on this special day!

And don't forget those half birthdays, celebrated six months after their real birthday. Mark the occasion with half of a birthday cake, half-sized candles, half-sized balloons, and half of a scoop of ice cream. If you choose to give presents, it could be half the number they normally would get, half their age in presents, or just a small one. You still are making the annual birthday the big one. The big difference between half birthdays and birthdays, if you will pardon the pun, is the half versus the half-nots.

The Most Important Birthday!

The most special birthday is open to interpretation, but I made a big deal of their tenth birthday. It was when they graduated into double digits, which is where most will live their complete lives. Other parents focus on thirteen or sixteen for their teenagers. But ten is something no one else does, so the kids get lots of admiration from their friends.

Since this was the biggest birthday, to me and to them, I did go all out. My daughter was allowed to get her ears pierced. This was two years before her mom got hers pierced, so we had to have a discussion about that. My son was allowed to get one video game that I had denied before. Both were rites of passage for them.

You can choose anything you want to make significant in their lives. Makeup, high-heeled shoes, and shaving the legs seem clichéd to a grown-up, but these are important things to girls.

Boys are a little harder. Friends of mine have taken the boys hunting, fishing, or to a professional sports game. The big thing we did was to rent a limousine for their birthdays, and allow them to invite a few friends. This was an expense that I was fortunate to have been able to afford, and what a difference it made, because most children of that age have never been in one. They were so proud of that moment, when their friends were oohing and aaahing over the spaciousness of the car.

They both got to choose the color. (My daughter chose white, and my son chose black.)

The entire day, though, is devoted to what the birthday kid wants. We listened to his or her music, ate at that child's favorite places, and did something he or she really wanted to do, such as go bowling, play laser tag, or go shopping.)

For entry into teenage-hood, I let them both drive the car, for the first time, in a parking lot. That's another story. If you do the same thing, be aware that the first time your kid steps on the brake will be jolting!

Picture Birthday

Ever rummage through all your family pictures and remember, with fondness, how your child's appearance has changed over the years? Adults generally look the same for long periods of time, but from the moment of birth to age eighteen, our children's faces change dramatically. On their birthday, plan on taking a picture, as you will do anyway, but instead of putting it in a drawer, an album, or online, place it side-by-side with all their other birthday photos. If you print them all the same size, you will need room for eighteen of them. I like to frame them in a 1-4-4-4-4-1 pattern. The one at the bottom should be his or her birth picture, and each row of four will group those particular years together, with the final photo at the top being his or her eighteenth birthday.

The progression, as I mentioned in the beginning of the book, that begins with a baby and ends when that baby becomes an adult, will be complete, This photographic memory lane will be something you will all cherish forever. Personally, I would make two of these, because you will never want to give up yours.

If you remember Dreamer Day from the January chapter and Favorite Day from the August chapter, this is a great way to combine your child's dreams, preferences, and pictures together in the frame, for a truly cherishable memory. It is something that your child's future spouse will be very impressed with.

Moving Day

In my professional career I have lived in several states and have, obviously, moved my family several times. These moves were usually accomplished with the help of a professional moving company, which packed up our possessions and moved them to our new home. The boxes they used to move us were fantastic. In fact, when we moved from Texas to Michigan, we had so many wardrobe boxes that I knew—like all parents know that a box, a pan, and a spoon are the best toys for little ones—that we could put these boxes together for a better purpose. Our new basement, the first one I'd ever had, inspired me to assemble several boxes together to build a fortress. I stood the tall wardrobe boxes at the corners, taped the regular boxes together (for crawling pleasure), cut out holes for windows, and then I gave the kids crayons and markers to decorate as they wanted. I was smart enough to place an old carpet under it, too, so it wasn't hard on their knees and made it easy for me to slide around. The kids loved it. Whenever they had friends over, the fortress was their play station. Dolls, blankets, and snacks were all pulled in, and the kids always had fun chases through the maze.

Daddy/Daughter Dinner and Father/Son Soiree

The Daddy/Daughter Dinners took place after the daddy/daughter dances at school, which began when my daughter was around eight years old. Many of the dads came for a couple hours after school, while a deejay played the popular songs of the time, as well as "The Chicken Dance" song and the Village People's "YMCA." After the dances, we headed to my daughter's favorite restaurant, the five-star Burger King, for some fries and a favorite drink.

My son never had dances at school, so we arranged to see a movie and then went out to *his* favorite five-star restaurant, McDonald's. It was a nice way to spend a few hours with my son, and we both got to check out the latest (at the time) animated movie and eat some fantastic popcorn.

Yes, thanks to both of my kids, I got to enjoy the best food money can buy.

I highly recommend continuing these traditions even after the kids have outgrown them, but instead of going for burgers and fries, take your kids to *your* favorite places so that they experience different settings, foods, atmospheres, and dinner-table discussions. My kids currently love Mexican restaurants and Japanese steak houses! These were the easiest restaurants to get them to expand their horizons (around age six), since the Mexican places served chips and salsa and that was already a dessert to them, while the Japanese steak houses, with the hibachi grills, were so entertaining that they enjoyed the spectacle. Of course, the food was good too, so those places set the stage for trying other places and then getting the kids to eat something other than chicken nuggets, hamburgers, hot dogs, or pizza.

Picnic Days

Picnic Days aren't really holidays for kids, per se, but rather, they are something we enjoyed doing when we found out that several school districts allow parents to visit at lunch. Make sure this is okay with your child's school's administration first, but once you have permission, you can stop by the school during lunchtime, bring a special lunch for you and your child, and eat inside or outside with him or her. You may also be able to meet your kid's friends and teachers, as well as see the lunchroom in action. The younger they are (between six and eight), the more they enjoy showing you off to their teachers and friends, especially if you bring McDonald's or Burger King, while everyone else eats cafeteria food. Check out your school's policy, and make this a nice picnic day!

Kids in the Kitchen Day

This is a day, of your choosing, when you can let the kids enjoy the experience of cooking for the family. Have your kids help in the kitchen, or maybe take the lead on some easy things, such as homemade pizza, a cake, hot dogs, sandwiches, popcorn, spaghetti, and toast, that aren't especially dangerous or complicated. Remember, these don't have to be intricate recipes. Homemade pizza can be the premade crust and pour on your favorite store bought sauce, some shredded mozzarella cheese, and presliced pepperoni slices. A cake is a little harder because of the mess with eggshells and flour, but it's a progression for them. One favorite was the premade cookies in a can you open and just slice and bake. It's the end result they will enjoy and remember as something *they* made and *you* ate!

Daddy Donut Day

Upon learning that both my kids loved donuts and wanted to go to the donut shop every week, I began restricting our donut shop visits to once per month. And each child could only have two donuts per visit. I found that, after we instituted the new restrictions, the kids knew exactly when a new month started. There were times, I selfishly admit, when I was craving donuts too, so a self-proclaimed Daddy Donut Day was definitely in order! It was an occasional treat that, unsurprisingly, they wanted me to exercise more frequently.

Bedtimes

I have previously stated that the one thing every child really understands is his or her age. Kids always know it, and it's a great way to get them to try new foods or eat some better foods. For example, you may ask, "How old are you?" When the answer comes back, "Four," you might then say, "Then please eat four more bites of your broccoli." It's amazing how easy that is and how it works . . . for a while. Be prepared to hear they are zero years old.

For bedtime, I often chose a time that correlated with the kids' ages. For four-year-olds, maybe the bedtime would be 8:04 pm. Then, as the child gets older, you might choose 8:15, 8:16, 8:27, 8:38, 8:49, 9:09. You get the idea. Pick a number that ends with the child's age, and use it to improve the daily schedule when you recognize that the children need to go to bed. Your kids will clock watch, like real professionals, and tell you when there's one minute remaining. They will even watch the second hand, but when it's time, they will go to bed.

I read to my kids every night. We read a variety of children's books, ranging from *Goodnight Moon, Children's Treasury of Virtues*, and *Bible Stories for Kids*. We also read chapter book series such as *The Magic School Bus, Junie B. Jones*, and *The Magic Tree House*. I loved the *I Spy* books because they taught the kids to focus and learn about many different objects. Find books that your kids like, and if they want you to read them over and over, that's fine, but make them participate in the reading. I used to put my finger under every word so they could simultaneously see and hear what I was reading, and when they were as young as two, they started to recognize a lot of words. While reading a story that your child likes, pause midsentence and have your child fill in the blanks occasionally.

Good Night and Good Morning Songs

At the end of each evening I sang a bedtime song to each of the kids. The one I chose came from *The Lawrence Welk Show*; it was the song the performers sang when they closed each show, and I made some changes at the end. It went like this:

> Good night, sleep tight, and pleasant dreams to you.
> Here's a wish and a prayer that every dream comes true.
> And now, till morning comes again, cover up, close your eyes,
>   and go to sleep.
> Good night!

After I had sung the song, I gave them as many hugs and kisses as the number of years they had lived on this earth.

I used the sign language gesture for "I love you," which is the thumb, index finger, and little finger spread apart. And then I asked them to form the same thing with their little hands. Like that, we joined our hands together, showing our love for each other. (It also continues as the sign language when they are waiting at the bus stop or with their friends as you drive by.)

Then, I finally pinched their soft noses and left.

This becomes very fun when you turn it around, on the days when you go to bed before your kids, and have them tuck *you* into bed. They will give you hugs and kisses for *your* age. Enjoy it while it lasts!

This tradition did go by the wayside, as each child ultimately told me that I didn't have to tuck him or her in anymore. But when I asked if the two of them remembered the words to the "Night Night" song, they both sang it back to me. Now, if I could get them to remember algebra that way, then I would really be a star.

Good Morning Song

For the times when you need to wake up your kids, if they are sleeping too long or have to go to school, I created this one:

> Good morning, little sleepy head.
> Jump up from your comfy bed.
> Rise up and meet the sun.
> Wake up and have some fun.

This is now the song that my teenaged children should be blasting from their radios and iPhones, because they sleep until two in the afternoon when they can. It was so much easier when they were young.

Daddy Diet Day

I never did this one, but with all the food that I ate during these holidays, I should have! I still am working on what day that be observed. Or better yet, what year(s)!

Epilogue

So there you have it, a whole year of holidays for kids. I hope this small collection of things you can do with your children creates the same wonderful memories for you that it did for me. Having a slightly warped sense of humor, and a willingness to invest a little time each month, will make a big difference in preparing and executing these ideas. They are not for everyone, and I strongly encourage you to keep your own family traditions alive and well. You may want to change some of your traditions to incorporate some that you have read here.

I remember someone once telling me that, as she was cooking a roast, her grown daughter asked, "Mom, why do you cut off the ends of the roast before cooking it?" The mother answered that this was the way her mother had taught her. The mother then wondered the same thing, and she asked *her* mother why. They were fortunate to have four living generations of family members. The great-grandmother said, "It was the only way I could fit it in the pan."

Traditions shouldn't simply be handed down. It's important to explain *why*. I wanted to preserve the enjoyment of childhood and to take advantage of the fun things we could share together. My kids have told me that they plan to do all my holidays, except March 4, Clean Up Your Room Day. They still think that it is cruel and unusual punishment. (I am betting it is the *first* one they implement!)

Another piece of advice: while they are young, get a small notebook and write down the funny things they say that make you laugh, the things they like at the time, what you did on these holidays, and your general observations. You will be amazed at how quickly we forget all the little things that make our kids who they are, and this notebook offers a better trip down memory lane than pictures alone. Tuck it away, and read it from time to time. That little trip is better than any picture you can pull out from a scrapbook. It also reinforces to the child what specific traits make him or her unique. It also shows your love for them.

I love to think of all the knowledge they have accumulated over the years. They continue to know about presidents, states, and holiday facts, but, more importantly, they see how they have changed and grown in their thoughts and looks.

I would like to thank my wife, Paula, who helped in arranging many of these events. She had her hands full with other things she did to make parties enjoyable, and maybe she will write a book about all the things she did with the kids, including: special parties, making and decorating cookies, painting pots, riding horses, teaching knitting or finger weaving, coloring books, making costumes for Halloween, and just being a good sport on so many of our adventures.

Finally, I also want to thank Taylor and Zachary, who inspired me to create all these holidays and give them memories that will last their lifetimes and mine.

I have been blessed to have a great family.
Charles Pascalar